FUNDAMENTALS OF LEGAL RESEARCH

Fifth Edition

and LEGAL RESEARCH ILLUSTRATED

Fifth Edition

Roy M. Mersky
Hyder Centennial Professor of Law
and Director of Research
Tarlton Law Library
University of Texas

J. Myron Jacobstein
Professor of Law Emeritus
and Law Librarian Emeritus
Stanford University

ASSIGNMENTS

Joyce Saltalamachia, Editor
Associate Professor of Law
and Library Director
New York Law School Library

Westbury, New York
THE FOUNDATION PRESS, INC.
1990

ISBN 0–88277–820–X

TO THE STUDENT:

To master the numerous nuances of legal research requires exercising the skills acquired through Fundamentals of Legal Research (5th ed.) or Legal Research Illustrated (5th ed.). That is the purpose of the Assignment Book.

We have provided numerous types of problems to introduce many aspects of legal research. The chapters in this assignment book correspond to the Fundamentals and Legal Research Illustrated.

Some problems specifically direct you to a particular source. Other problems require you to choose a specific title within a series or multi-volume work. Another group of problems is less directive as to the resource which may answer the question. This variety of assignments is provided to exercise two skills: an ability to choose among different approaches to resolving a legal problem and an ability to glean the most information when limited to a particular resource.

Keep in mind four criteria when choosing among resources. First, what is the scope of a particular title? Does this title exclusively cover the information you desire or will you have to deal with superfluous information in order to answer the problem? Secondly, how is a particular title arranged? Does the title provide a "How to Use" guide? Thirdly, how is the title you have chosen to answer the question indexed? Is there a combination of tables and indexes which provide a comprehensive approach to the information in the title or is access limited? Finally, how current is the information provided in the title? Do you need current information to answer the question? How is the information updated--through cumulative supplements, pocketparts, replacement volumes, looseleaf pages or new editions. Is the indexing appropriately current to the form of updating?

Although these issues appear generic, their application to a problem can aid you as you pursue the course of study as outlined in the Fundamentals or Legal Research Illustrated and the Assignment Book. If you are not comfortable in using certain types of legal materials following your readings in Fundamentals or Legal Research Illustrated and classroom lectures, apply the scope, arrangement, index and update strategy. This analysis is particularly useful having the book(s) in hand. A few moments in the library using this approach can save hours of frustration.

We have provided many duplicate types of problems so your classmates will not have to share one particular book. Although you may not be doing the same problems, the questions are designed to be balanced and to exercise identical or similar skills. There are no "trick questions." If you find you are laboring over a particular question longer than fifteen minutes, seek assistance from your instructor or librarian. Maintain a detailed record of your research strategy (or pathfinder). When you encounter obstacles in your research, reviewing the pathfinder with an instructor or librarian can facilitate clarifying your confusion.

Problem solving in the legal profession involves gathering the operative facts, identifying the legal issues, researching the legal issues and resolving the legal issues through effective writing by applying the law to the factual setting. Each of these steps builds upon the other. Successful lawyering requires analysis and research. Your first year of law school introduces each step. Equal attention must be given to each process component if you are to be successful as a lawyer. Many times poor analysis or confused writing is the result of ineffectual research. Diligence in using these assignments in conjunction with the Fundamentals of Legal Research or Legal Research Illustrated provides you with a sound foundation in the legal process.

A problem book of this magnitude is the result of intellectual and clerical hard work. We particularly thank our editor Professor Joyce Saltalamachia, Associate Professor and Director of the Law Library at the New York Law School.

Professor Saltalamachia wishes to gratefully acknowledge the invaluable assistance of Loretta Goldstein of the New York Law School Library in the final preparation of this manuscript. Thanks also goes to Delores Taylor for her typing services.

We close by reiterating our final thoughts in the previous edition of this problem book. Our greatest reward is in the appreciation and professional fulfillment we enjoy in knowing that many lawyers have gained from this workbook the skills necessary to solve the law's mystery.

J. Myron Jacobstein
Stanford University School of Law

Roy M. Mersky
University of Texas School of Law

Stanford
Austin
May, 1990

TABLE OF CONTENTS

CHAPTER 4

FEDERAL COURT DECISIONS

ASSIGNMENT 1
EXAMINATION OF UNITED STATES REPORTS

Questions:

A. Using the early volumes of United States Reports and the latest edition of A Uniform System of Citation, find the United States Reports (U.S.) volume number for the following nominative reports. Put your answer in proper citation form.

1. 8 Wheaton
2. 6 Cranch
3. 20 Wallace
4. 5 Peters
5. 24 Howard
6. 12 Wallace
7. 9 Cranch
8. 12 Wheaton
9. 8 Peters
10. 3 Dallas
11. 11 Wheaton
12. 2 Black
13. 21 Howard
14. 13 Wallace
15. 8 Cranch
16. 4 Dallas
17. 1 Howard
18. 12 Peters

19. 7 Wallace

20. 20 Howard

B. Using the latest edition of <u>A Uniform System of Citation</u> and <u>United States Reports</u> (U.S.), find the names of the following cases and cite them properly in your answer.

1. 340 U.S. 581
2. 293 U.S. 388
3. 283 U.S. 494
4. 288 U.S. 290
5. 300 U.S. 5
6. 306 U.S. 451
7. 315 U.S. 32
8. 397 U.S. 337
9. 399 U.S. 66
10. 378 U.S. 368
11. 358 U.S. 133
12. 367 U.S. 643
13. 402 U.S. 415
14. 401 U.S. 154
15. 399 U.S. 66
16. 397 U.S. 254
17. 396 U.S. 435
18. 395 U.S. 752
19. 394 U.S. 576
20. 372 U.S. 335

ASSIGNMENT 2
UNITED STATES REPORTS - RELATED MATERIALS

Method:

For each of the citations to the official United States Reports (U.S.), locate the unofficial parallel citation in the West's Supreme Court Reporter (S. Ct.) and the United States Supreme Court Reports, Lawyers' Edition (L. Ed.).

Questions:

1. 358 U.S. 133
2. 402 U.S. 415
3. 399 U.S. 66
4. 394 U.S. 576
5. 372 U.S. 335
6. 340 U.S. 581
7. 293 U.S. 388
8. 288 U.S. 290
9. 300 U.S. 5
10. 306 U.S. 451
11. 315 U.S. 32
12. 378 U.S. 368
13. 376 U.S. 665
14. 380 U.S. 451
15. 386 U.S. 237
16. 390 U.S. 62
17. 395 U.S. 100
18. 405 U.S. 34
19. 406 U.S. 164
20. 411 U.S. 1

ASSIGNMENT 3
FEDERAL CASES

Questions:

A. Using the set Federal Cases (F. Cas.) and the latest edition of A Uniform System of Citation, find the name of the following cases and properly cite them.

1. Federal Case Number 358
2. Federal Case Number 18,210
3. Federal Case Number 7,881
4. Federal Case Number 9,317
5. Federal Case Number 2,865
6. Federal Case Number 1,424
7. Federal Case Number 2,344
8. Federal Case Number 3,555
9. Federal Case Number 6,994
10. Federal Case Number 13,753
11. Federal Case Number 9,596
12. Federal Case Number 11,825
13. Federal Case Number 8,260
14. Federal Case Number 14,249
15. Federal Case Number 15,959

B. Using the Table of Citations in the Digest volume of Federal Cases (F. Cas.), locate the following decisions. Put your answer in proper citation form. [Instructions: Locate the digest volume to the set Federal Cases. Within it is a Table of Citations (these are on colored pages in the edition used by the editor) listing reporters alphabetically. A parallel citation is given to the Federal Case Number.]

1. Fish. Pat. Cas. 483
2. 19 Int. Rev. Rec. 108
3. 5 Dill. 549
4. 1 Leg. Gaz. Rep. 279

5. 12 O.G. 1026

6. 1 McLean 120

7. Abb. Adm. 529

8. 7 Biss. 426

9. 8 N.B.R. 525

10. 1 Lowell 91

11. 2 Sumn. 108

12. 2 McLean 464

13. 1 Bond 1

14. 4 Brewst. 250

15. Spear, Extrad. (2d ed.) 451

ASSIGNMENT 4
DRILL PROBLEMS AND THEME PROBLEMS

Drill Problem I:

A. Nominative Reports

1. Using the early volumes of the United States Reports give the official U.S. volume number citation for each of the following:
(a) 1 Cranch
(b) 7 Wheaton
(c) 4 Dallas

2. Compare the volume designated 6 Cranch with 400 U.S. and answer the following questions:
(a) Contrast the features of the two volumes.
(b) Provide the full citation for the case which is printed in part on page 100 of each volume.

B. United States Reports - Parallel Citation:

Using the parallel citations tables in the West's Supreme Court Reporter and the United States Supreme Court Reports, Lawyers Edition, find the parallel citations for each of the following cases:

1. Fuller v. Oregon, 417 U.S. 40 (1974)

2. Hanson v. Denckla, 357 U.S. 235 (1958)

3. Ring v. U.S., 419 U.S. 18 (1974)

4. Piascik v. U.S., 434 U.S. 1062 (1978)

C. Lower Federal Court Cases

1. Using volume 425 of the Federal Reporter, Second Series, answer the following:
   (a) Who was the Circuit Justice for the Fifth Circuit?
   (b) Give the correct cite for the case of Boyk v. Mitchell.
   (c) Cite the case that defines "blatantly lawless."
   (d) Cite any cases that construe 25 U.S.C. 357.
   (e) How many headnotes in Rhodes v. Craven?

2. Using volume 300 of Federal Supplement, answer the following:
   (a) Who is the Chief Judge of the U.S. Customs Court?
   (b) Give the correct citation for Bjarsch v. DiFalco.
   (c) What case defines the term "motorboat"?
   (d) What article and section of the Tennessee Constitution are construed in this volume?

(e) What is the docket number of Arrow Transportation Co?

3. Using volume 200 of Federal Reporter answer the following:
   (a) What courts are covered by this volume?
   (b) Who was the Chief Justice of the First Circuit Court of Appeals?
   (c) On what page does the case of Berardini v. Tocci appear?
   (d) Are any California statutes construed? Which one?
   (e) What case begins at p. 859?

4. Using Federal Cases, answer the following:
   (a) Give the full citation of the following cases:
      (1) F. Cas. No. 5
      (2) F. Cas. No. 25
   (b) Give the Federal Case Number of the following cases:
      (1) Wood v. Wells
      (2) Reid. v. Rochereau

Drill Problem II

A. Nominative Reports

1. Give the full citation for the following cases. Using the latest edition of A Uniform System of Citation put your answer in proper citation form.
   (a) The case in volume 4 of the reports of John William Wallace at page 189.
   (b) The case located in volume 16 of the reports of Richard Peters at page one.
   (c) Using volume 2 of the reports of Henry Wheaton, state when Bushrod Washington became Associate Justice of the Supreme Court.

2. Making your answer complete and concise, compare volume 6 of Benjamin C. Howard's reports with volume 380 of the United States Reports in the following respects:
   (a) Contrast the features of the two.
   (b) Provide the full citation for the case appearing on page 163 of each volume.

B. Find the following cases in the West's Supreme Court Reporter and the United States Supreme Court Reports, Lawyers' Edition by using their parallel citation tables. State volume and page.

1. Briscoe v. Bell, 432 U.S. 404 (1977).

2. Zwicker v. Boll, 391 U.S. 353 (1968).

3. Miami Herald Publishing Co. v. Tornillo, 481 U.S. 241 (1974).

C. Lower Federal Court Cases

1. Using volume 617 of the Federal Reporter, Second Series answer the following:
   (a) Who was the Chief Judge of the Second Circuit:
   (b) Using the latest edition of A Uniform System of Citation, give the correct citation for Narenji v. Civiletti.
   (c) Cite the case defining "arbitrary."
   (d) How many cases in this volume came from the Third Circuit?
   (e) What case construed the American Bar Association's Code of Professional Responsibility? Properly cite it.

2. Using volume 484 of the Federal Supplement, answer the following:
   (a) On what court did George H. Barlow sit prior to his death?
   (b) Using the latest edition of A Uniform System of Citation, give the citation for the case defining "controversial."
   (c) What case interpreted the Wisconsin Constitution?
   (d) Who represented the plaintiff in Hawkins-El v. Williams?

3. Using Federal Cases, answer the following:
   (a) Give the full citation of Federal Case Number 3,914.
   (b) Find the federal case number of Ross v. Peaslee. Properly cite the case in your answer.

Drill Problem III

A. Nominative Reports

1. Give the full citation for the following cases. Using the latest edition of A Uniform System of Citation, put your answer in proper cite form.
   (a) The case located in volume 20 of the reports of Benjamin C. Howard at page 486.
   (b) The case located in volume 2 of the reports of Henry Wheaton at page 248.
   (c) A case located in volume 4 of the reports of John William Wallace which deals with prisoners of war.
2. Making your answer complete and concise compare volume 16 of Richard Peters' reports with volume 418 of the United States Reports in the following respects:
   (a) Contrast the features of the two.
   (b) Provide the full citation for the case appearing on page 153 of each volume.

B. Find the following cases in the West's Supreme Court Reporter and the United States Supreme Court Reports, Lawyers Edition by using their parallel citation tables. State volume and page.

1. Blount v. Rizzi, 400 U.S. 410 (1971).

2. Reading Co. v. Brown, 391 U.S. 471 (1968).

3. Mandel v. Bradley, 432 U.S. 173 (1977).

C. Lower Federal Court Cases

1. Using volume 637 of the Federal Reporter, Second Series answer the following:
   (a) Each of the Justices of the Supreme Court serves as a Circuit Justice for one of the federal circuits. As of the time of volume 637, who sat as the Circuit Justice for the Fourth Circuit?
   (b) Using the latest edition of A Uniform System of Citation, give the correct citation for the case interpreting Fed. R. Civ. P. 24(a).
   (c) Give the correct citation for the case defining "carry."
   (d) What states or political subdivisions are in the Third Circuit?
   (e) Who dissented in a case involving Roadway Express, Inc.?

2. Using volume 497 of the Federal Supplement, answer the following:
   (a) How many cases were decided by the District Court of Puerto Rico?
   (b) Cite the case which defines "citizen."
   (c) Cite the case interpreting the Alabama Code.
   (d) What judge decided United States v. Wenzel?

3. Using Federal Cases, answer the following:
   (a) Give the full citation of Federal Case Number 1,408.
   (b) Find the Federal case of Clark v. Bininger. Is there an opinion printed in Federal Cases?

Theme Problem I:

Roe v. Wade was one of the most talked about decisions of the past decade. It can be found at 410 U.S. 113 (1973). Locate the case and answer the following questions:

1. Who wrote the majority opinion?

2. Is there a concurring opinion or opinions? If so, who wrote it, or them?

3. Is there a dissenting opinion or opinions? If so, who wrote it, or them?

4. What is the date of decision?

5. How many headnotes precede the case?

6. Who is Wade?

7. Who reargued the case for appellants?

8. Roe v. Wade can also be found at 93 S. Ct. 705 and 35 L. Ed. 2d 147.

Look up each of these and answer the following:
(a) How many headnotes in each?
(b) What else is different about the opinions?
(c) Examine the "extras" in each volume: front matter, tables, and indexes, etc. List what's available in each.
(d) Are there any annotations in the United States Supreme Court Reports, Lawyers' Edition? If so, examine one.

9. At 410 U.S. 155, the Court cites Shapiro v. Thompson, 394 U.S. 618 (1969). Locate that case.
(a) Answer questions 1-5 above for it.
(b) Locate the same (Shapiro) case in West's Supreme Court Reporter and United States Supreme Court Reports, Lawyers' Edition, 2d. Give the citations and answer questions 8(a) - 8(d) for this case.

10. Also at 410 U.S. 155, the Court cites Sherbert v. Verner, 374 U.S. 398 (1963). Locate that case.
(a) Answer questions 1-5 for it.
(b) Locate the same case in West's Supreme Court Reporter and United States Supreme Court Reports, Lawyers' Edition, 2d. Give the Citations and answer the questions 8(a) - 8(d) for that case.

11. At 410 U.S. 155 the Court cites Crossen v. Attorney General, 344 F. Supp. 587(E.D. Ky. 1970). Locate that case.
(a) In what court does it arise?
(b) Does it have headnotes? How many?
(c) Who wrote this opinion?
(d) Does this volume have a case table? Key Number Digest section?

12. At 410 U.S. 158 the Court cites Montana v. Rogers, 278 F.2d 68 (CA7, 1960).
(a) What does (CA7, 1960) mean?
(b) Answer the questions posed in 11(a) - 11(d) for the case.

13. How could one determine if the Supreme Court has decided any cases on abortion in its current term? Has it?

Theme Problem II

Gideon v. Wainwright was a case of importance in setting our standards for criminal justice. It can be found at 372 U.S. 335 (1963). Locate the case and answer the following questions:

1. What is the date of decision?

2. Who wrote the majority opinions?

3. Is there a concurring opinion or opinions? Who wrote it, or them?

4. Is there a dissenting opinion or opinions? Who wrote it, or them?

5. Where did the case originate?

6. Who argued the case for Gideon?

7. Are there any headnotes?

8. What is the result?

9. Gideon v. Wainwright can also be found in the West's Supreme Court Reporter and United States Supreme Court Reports, Lawyers' Edition, 2d.
   (a) Locate it, give the citations to the unofficial reporters.
   (b) How many headnotes in each?
   (c) Is there any difference in the opinions?
   (d) Examine the "extras" available in each volume: front matter, tables and indexes, etc. List what is available in each.
   (e) Are there any annotations in the United States Supreme Court Reports, Lawyers' Edition? If so, examine one.

10. At 372 U.S. 338 the Court cites Betts v. Brady. What is the official citation for Betts? Locate that case and answer questions 1-5 for that case.

11. At 372 U.S. page 346, Justice Douglas cites The Slaughter House Cases, 16 Wall. 36. What other designation does 16 Wall. have? Locate that case and answer questions 105 for it.

12. What does Gideon v. Wainwright overrule? Find the West's Supreme Court Reporter and United States Supreme Court Reports, Lawyers' Edition citation for that case.

13. At 372 U.S. 351 in footnote 5, Justice Harlan cites Henderson v. Bannan, 256 F.2d 363 (C.A. 6th Cir. 1958). Locate that case:
   (a) What does C.A. 6th Cir. mean?
   (b) How many headnotes does the decision have?
   (c) Who wrote the opinion?
   (d) In what court did it originate?
   (e) Could this decision be found anywhere else?

14. How would one determine if the Supreme Court dealt with any cases concerning a criminal defendant's right to counsel this term? Has it?

Theme Problem III

Among the more controversial opinions you will read this year is that of Justice Cardozo in Palsgraf v. Long Island R.R. Co., 248 N.Y. 339, 162 N.E. 99 (1928). There, in determining whether a woman on the platform of a train station could recover for injuries she received due to an explosion, Cardozo dealt at length with the topics of duty and foreseeability.

A. Martinez v. California, 444 U.S. 277 (1980) cites to Palsgraf. Answer the following with reference to Martinez.

1. Who wrote the opinion?

2. Who represented the Martinez family at oral argument?

3. Did any justice write a separate opinion?

4. What was the date of the decision?

5. Was Palsgraf necessary to the decision of the court?

B. Martinez can also be found at 62 L. Ed. 2d 481 and 100 S. Ct. 553. Compare and contrast the treatment given the case in these reports and in the official version.

C. Palsgraf is cited in 452 F.2d at page 178.

1. Give the full citation for the case citing Palsgraf.

2. Which headnote(s) are supported by Palsgraf.

3. Who was the Chief Judge of the Seventh Circuit where the case was decided?

4. What states are served by the Seventh Circuit?

5. How many cases in 452 F.2d came to the Seventh Circuit from Wisconsin?

6. What case in 452 F.2d defines the term "transmission?" Properly cite it.

7. Who wrote the opinion in the case cited in Question C.6?

8. What case in 452 F.2d cites to 21 U.S.C.A. sec. 355(h)? Properly cite it.

Theme Problem IV

Sherwood v. Walker, 66 Mich. 568, 33 N.W. 919 (1887) represents one of the fundamental cases dealing with mutual mistake in the making of contracts. In his dissenting opinion, Justice Sherwood of the Michigan Supreme Court attempts to distinguish Allen v. Hammond, 11 Pet. 63, on which the majority relies.

A. Locate Allen and answer the following questions which relate to it:

1. Give its full citation.

2. Who wrote the majority opinion?

3. Did any justices write separate opinions?

4. Who was Chief Justice at the time of the decision?

5. Who argued for the appellee?

B. The same case can be found at 9 L. Ed. 633.

1. Compare and contrast the two reports.

2. Why does the case not appear in West's Supreme Court Reporter?

C. Sherwood is discussed in 621 F.2d at 1349.

1. Give the full citation of the case which cites Sherwood.

2. For which headnote is Sherwood cited?

3. Who wrote the opinion?

4. Who dissented?

5. Who was chief Judge of the Fifth Circuit at the time?

6. At the time, what states were located in the Fifth Circuit?

7. How many cases arose in West Virginia that were reported in 621 F.2d?

8. What case in 621 F.2d cites the Rules of the Supreme Court of the United States?

CHAPTER 5

STATE COURT DECISIONS AND THE NATIONAL REPORTER SYSTEM

ASSIGNMENT 1
COURT REPORTS

Questions:

1. The opinions of what courts in your state are published in any form--official or unofficial?

2. List the current official and unofficial reports for your state.

3. In what form do the official decisions in your state first appear, i.e., slip opinion, advance sheet, bound volume?

4. Compare a current volume of the California Reporter and a current volume of the Pacific Reporter. The opinions of which California court are duplicated?

5. Compare a current volume of the New York Supplement and a current volume of the North Eastern Reporter. The opinions of what New York court are duplicated in both reporters?

6. Examine a current volume of the National Reporter System regional unit which includes your state. Find the "Table of Contents" and list the material contained in this volume.

7. Examine volume 484 P.2d. Cite the pages of the two tables of cases which cite Ridell v. Rhay.

8. Give the complete citation to a case in 189 N.W.2d which construes the following statute:

   North Dakota Century Code 1-02-10

9. Give the citation to a case and the page number of the case in 183 S.E.2d which defines the word "war."

10. Examine the Key Number digest section of volume 470 S.W.2d. Give the subject, key number, and citation to the first case digested.

11. Examine the case in volume 273 N.E.2d at page 252. Answer the following:

    (a) What is the name of the case?
    (b) What is the docket number?
    (c) What is the name of the court?

12. Examine the case of E. & E. Newman v. Hallock at 281 A.2d 544. Answer the following:

    (a) What is the official state report citation for this case, if any?
    (b) How many different key numbers are listed in the headnotes of this case?

13. Examine the case of De Palma v. State, 185 S.E.2d 53. Answer the following:

    (a) Headnotes 3, 4, and 5 are discussed on which page of the opinion?
    (b) Syllabus 4(b) of the court is discussed on which page of the opinion?

14. Cases in the National Reporter System units appear first in advance sheet form.

    (a) Is the pagination in the advance sheets the same as that in the bound volume?
    (b) Will the text of the cases found in the advance sheets always be the same as that in the bound volumes which replace them?

15. The Key Number Digest section is located at the end of each bound volume of the National Reporter system. Where is the Key Number Digest section located in the National Reporter System advance sheets?

16. Examine volume 113 A.2d. Cite the pages of the two tables of cases which cite Bata v. Hill.

17. Give the complete citation to a case in volume 97 N.E.2d which construes Article 8, sec. 4 of the Ohio Constitution.

18. Give the citation to a case in 106 Cal. Rptr. which defines the word "revolver," and the page number on which the definition is found.

19. Examine the Key Number digest section of volume 201 N.Y.S.2d. Give the subject, Key Number, and citation to the first case digested.

20. Examine the case in volume 89 So. 2d at page 459. Answer the following:

    (a) What is the name of the case?
    (b) What is the docket number?
    (c) What is the name of the court?

21. Examine the case of State v. Waid at 67 P.2d 647. Answer the following:

    (a) Is the official state report citation given for this case?
    (b) How many different Key Numbers are listed in the headnotes of this case?

22. Examine the case of United States Cold Storage Corp. v. Stolinski, 96 N.W.2d 408. Answer the following:

    (a) Headnotes 8, 9 are discussed on what page?
    (b) Syllabus 2 of the court is found on what page?

23. Examine the case of Green v. State, 209 S.W.2d 195. Answer the following:

    (a) In what court was the appeal heard?
    (b) What were the names of the attorneys for the appellant?
    (c) What was the name of the judge who wrote the opinion of the court?
    (d) What was the name of the judge who wrote the opinion on the appellant's motion for rehearing?

ASSIGNMENT 2
PARALLEL CITATIONS

Method:

Using the National Reporter System Blue Books and Supplements, provide the parallel citation for each citation given below.

Questions:

1. 159 Ala. 410
2. 20 Cal. App. 252
3. 110 Ind. 294
4. 97 S.C. 261
5. 86 Tex. Cr. 620
6. 340 Mass. 334
7. 75 N.J. Super. 192
8. 198 Pa. Super. 169
9. 69 Wash. 2d 144
10. 83 Nev. 1

ASSIGNMENT 3
USE OF THE TABLE OF CASES

Method:

Using the table of cases in the reporter volumes shown, provide the proper pagination.

Questions:

1. Adler v. Bush Terminal Co., 291 N.Y.S.
2. Hensel v. Cahill, 116 A.2d
3. State ex rel. Harbage v. Ferguson, 36 N.E.2d
4. Burt v. Munger, 23 N.W.2d
5. Handley v. Jackson, 51 P.
6. Strickland v. Johnson, 197 S.E.
7. Savage v. Olson, 9 So. 2d
8. Owens v. Daniel, 16 S.W.2d
9. Bodrey v. Bodrey, 161 S.E.2d
10. Weddle v. Cox, 394 P.2d

ASSIGNMENT 4
USE OF VOLUME DIGEST

Method:

Using the digest to the reporter volumes shown, provide the citation to the appropriate case.

Questions:

1. A case in 110 A.2d concerning the liability of warehousemen to the owners of goods which are lost, destroyed, or damaged.

2. A case in 71 Cal. Rptr. concerning certainty and definiteness as requisites of a statute.

3. A case in 218 N.Y.S.2d concerning the effect of old age on the testamentary capacity to make a will.

4. A case in 18 N.E.2d concerning acts or conduct constituting comtempt of court.

5. A case in 538 S.W.2d concerning limiting the time or scope of argument of counsel.

6. A case in 223 So.2d concerning the care required and liability in general of inn keepers.

7. A case in 472 P.2d concerning the nature and theory of the right of subrogation.

8. A case in 308 A.2d concerning injury to or destruction of fish.

9. A case in 154 N.W.2d concerning discretion of the court relating to new trial.

10. A case in 59 N.E.2d concerning nature of a constructive trust.

ASSIGNMENT 5
USE OF THE TABLE OF STATUTES CONSTRUED

Method:

Using the table of statutes construed for the reporter volumes shown, provide the citation to the appropriate case.

Questions:

1. Uniform Fraudulent Conveyance Act, sec. 4 (112 A.2d)
2. 26 U.S.C.A. §1033 (72 Cal. Rptr.)
3. U.S. CONST., amend. I (203 N.Y.S.2d)
4. Ohio General Codes, sec. 26 (65 N.E.2d)
5. Uniform Commercial Code, 2-201 (2) (536 S.W.2d)
6. Louisiana Code of Criminal Procedure, art. 920 (308 So. 2d)
7. U.S. CONST. art. IV, §1 (535 P.2d)
8. South Dakota Compiled Laws, 1-26-36 (195 N.W.2d)
9. N.Y. TOWN LAW §268 (2) (229 N.Y.S.2d)
10. Pa. RULES CRIM. P. 150 (340 A.2d)

ASSIGNMENT 6
USE OF WORDS AND PHRASES

Method:

Using the Words and Phrases section of the reporter volumes shown, provide the citation to the appropriate case.

Questions:

1. "Employer," 85 Cal. Rptr.
2. "Direct Evidence," 83 N.E.2d.
3. "Enclosed Structure," 534 S.W.2d.
4. "Child," 108 P.2d.
5. "Mutual," 152 N.W.2d.
6. "Duress," 49 N.E.2d.
7. "Unfitness," 128 N.W.2d.
8. "Domicile," 85 N.E.2d.
9. "Reasonable," 204 N.W.2d.
10. "Lapsed Legacy," 173 N.Y.S.2d.

ASSIGNMENT 7
THEME PROBLEMS AND DRILL PROBLEMS

Theme Problem I:

A. Brown v. Board of Education is cited at 358 A.2d 835. Locate this decision and answer the following questions about the case that contains it.

1. What is the name and citation of the case which cites Brown?
2. Which is the official citation?
3. Who represented defendant Evans?
4. If you wanted to find other cases in this volume dealing with the same point for which Brown is cited, how would you do it?
5. What states does this reporter cover?
6. Give the name and citation of any case in this volume that mentions the Constitution of New Hampshire.
7. Give the name and citation of a case in this volume that defines "startling event."
8. Who was the chief justice of the Maine Supreme Judicial Court when Rybeck was rendered?

B. Brown v. Board of Education is also cited at 223 S.E.2d 617 in a dissent. Locate this citation and answer the following questions concerning the case in which the citation is found:

1. What is the name and citation of the case?
2. Is there an official citation given? If so, what is it?
3. Who wrote the dissent that cited Brown?
4. Why does no headnote cover the part of the opinion in which the citation of Brown occurs?
5. What states does this reporter cover?
6. Give the name and citation of any case in this volume that cites the North Carolina Code of Judicial Conduct.
7. Who was the chief judge of the Georgia Court of Appeals at the time this case was decided?

Chapter 5

Theme Problem II:

A. Roe v. Wade cites the case found at 354 S.W.2d 161. Locate this case and answer the following questions concerning it:

1. Give the correct name and citation of the case.

2. Note there is no official citation. List two reasons why this may be.

3. Who represented the state?

4. What is the result?

5. If you wanted to find other cases in this volume on the topic covered under headnote seven, how could you do it?

6. Give the names and citations of any cases in this volume that interpret the Kentucky Constitution.

7. Give the name and citation of a case in this volume that defines the term "gondola."

8. Who was the presiding judge of the Kansas City (Missouri) Court of Appeals when this case was decided?

B. Roe v. Wade also cites to 250 So. 2d 857. Locate that case and answer the following questions concerning it:

1. Give the correct name and citation of this case.

2. List the counsel who participated.

3. List any concurring opinions.

4. What is the result?

5. If one wanted to locate other cases in this volume that deal with the point covered in headnote 1, how could one do it?

6. What other states are covered by this reporter?

7. Give the names and citations of any cases in this volume that mention the Florida Code of Ethics.

8. Where in this volume could one find the opinion in Rachal v. Rachal?

9. Give the name and citation of a case in this volume that defines the term "religious."

10. Name the person who was presiding judge of the Louisiana 3rd Circuit Court of Appeals as of the decision in Walsingham.

Chapter 5

Theme Problem III:

Palsgraf v. Long Island R. Co. is located at 162 N.E. 99.

A. Answer the following with regard to Palsgraf:

1. What is the citation in the official reporter?

2. Give the full names of the three dissenting judges.

3. Who represented the railroad?

4. What other jurisdictions are reported in this volume?

B. Palsgraf is referred to at 350 N.Y.S.2d 651. Answer the following with regard to that case:

1. Give its full citation, indicating on what page the court cites to Palsgraf.

2. For what reason does it refer to Cardozo?

3. Cite another case in the volume which defines "motorcycle."

4. What case in the volume deals with the first amendment to the United States Constitution?

Theme Problem IV:

A. Sherwood v. Walker can be found at 33 N.W. 919. Look at the case and answer the following questions:

1. What is the citation in the official reporter:

2. What other jurisdictions are represented in the same volume?

B. Sherwood is referred to at 294 N.W. 708. Answer the following questions relating to that case:

1. What is the full citation?

2. How does the organization of its headnotes differ from Sherwood?

3. What is the full name of the justice who wrote the opinion?

C. A later Michigan case extends the concept of mistake from a settlement agreement to vacating a consent judgment at 185 N.W.2d 64.

1. Who represented the City of Warren in that case?

2. What case in the same volume defines "abuse of discretion?"

3. How many cases in the volume come from South Dakota?

Chapter 5

Drill Problem I:

Use the National Reporter System. Answer as concisely as possible.

1. Parallel Citations. Give the National Reporter citation for the following cases. Use the National Reporter Blue Books.
   (a) 363 Mo. 442
   (b) 264 Ind. 313
   (c) 280 Md. 332

2. Features of the National Reporter System volumes.
   (a) Table of Cases. Using the volume shown, provide the page citation for the listed cases.
      (i) In 477 S.W.2d, Travelers Ins.Co. v. Speer.
      (ii) In 520 P.2d, State v. Clark.
      (iii) In 290 N.E.2d, Slocum v. Fire and Police Comm. of City of East Peoria.
   (b) Statues Construed. Using the volume shown, provide the page citation to the case that cites the following statute.
      (i) In 344 A.2d. Rule 803(6) of the U.S. Federal Rules of Evidence.
      (ii) In 568 S.W.2d, Art. 6, §9 of the Tennessee Constitution.
   (c) Words and Phrases. Using the volume shown, provide the page citation for the case that defines the following terms:
      (i) In 241 S.E.2d, "Suit at Law"
      (ii) In 349 So. 2d, "As the Case May Be"

Drill Problem II:

Use the National Reporter System. Answer as concisely as possible.

1. Parallel Citations. Give the National Reporter citation for the following cases. Use the National Reporter Blue Books.
   (a) 76 Cal. App. 3d 302
   (b) 240 Ga. 479
   (c) 85 Idaho 226

2. Features of the National Reporter System volumes.
   (a) Table of Cases. Using the volume shown, provide the page citation for the listed cases.
      (i) In 167 S.E.2d, Young v. State.
      (ii) In 232 N.E.2d, Zoppo Co. V. Com.
      (iii) In 539 P.2d, Zylstra v. Piva.
   (b) Statutes Construed. Using the volume shown, provide the page citation of the case that cites the following statute.
      (i) In 583 P.2d, Kansas Statutes Annotated 21-3302.
      (ii) In 269 N.W.2d, A.B.A. Code of Professional Responsibility, D-R 5-104(A).
   (c) Words and Phrases. Using the volume shown, provide the page citation for the case that defines the following terms:
      (i) In 565 S.W.2d, "Liberty"
      (ii) In 380 N.E.2d, "Or"

Chapter 5

Drill Problem III:

A. Parallel Citations. Using the National Reporter Blue Books, give the National Reporter citation for the following cases:

1. 187 Kan. 458

2. 10 N.Y.2d 859

3. 4 N.C. App. 652

B. Using the volume indicated, provide the full citation for the following cases:

1. In 364 S.2d, a case in which the Shell Oil Company was the defendant.

2. In 213 S.E.2d, a case in which George Vick was the defendant.

3. In 564 S.W.2d, a case construing the Texas Election Code.

4. In 237 N.W.2d, a case defining "Criminal Assault."

5. In 399 N.E.2d, a case dealing with Fines.

6. In 582 P.2d, a case from Utah involving a sugar company.

Drill Problem IV:

A. Parallel Citations. Using the National Reporter Blue Books, give the National Reporter citation for the following cases:

1. 141 Ga. App. 678

2. 265 Ind. 616

3. 115 R.I. 303

B. Using the volume indicated, provide the full citation for the following cases:

1. A case in 424 A.2d, in which Barry Brann sued the state of Maine.

2. A case in 415 N.E.2d, in which John Green was the defendant.

3. A case in 283 N.W.2d, construing Mich. Comp. Laws §430.53.

4. A case in 614 P.2d, defining "Arms."

5. A case in 273 S.E.2d, dealing with Products Liability.

6. A case in 621 P.2d, dealing with a taxicab company, decided by

the Nevada Supreme Court.

CHAPTER 6

DIGESTS FOR COURT REPORTS

ASSIGNMENT 1
USE OF THE AMERICAN DIGEST SYSTEM

Method:

Using the indexes of the Decennial Digest specified at the beginning of each problem, carry out the following six steps in accord with the example given in the beginning of the problems:

(1) Answer the question with a "yes" or "no," basing your answer on information found in the specified digest.

(2) List the Topic and Key Numbers(s) under which the digest paragraph was found.

(3) Using the Topic Outline, what is the specific subject of the Topic and Key Number(s)?

(4) Using the latest edition of A Uniform System of Citation for proper form, give the case name and full citation to which the digest paragraph you located applies.

(5) Are there any cases in the first ten volumes of the General Digest Sixth Series under the same Topic and Key Number(s) as found in (2) supra? Answer with either the specific volume number(s) or the word "none."

(6) Give the corresponding or most nearly similar Century Digest (1658-1896) Topic and Section Number for the Topic and Key Number in (2) supra.

Example:

QUESTION: Use Fifth Decennial. Mr. Ned Lee of Webster County, Mississippi, sued the Memphis, Tennessee Publishing Company, a Delaware Corporation, for damages arising out of an allegedly defamatory and libelous article published by the defendant. Service of process was effected against, among others, the Secretary of State of the State of Mississippi. Defendant moved for dismissal based on lack of jurisdiction, stating it was not "present" within the state, that it was not doing business within the State of Mississippi, and that (by implication) it would violate due process of law contrary to Section 1 of Article XIV of the U.S. Constitution to subject defendant to local jurisdiction. Should the defendant prevail?

ANSWER:

(1) Yes.
(2) Constitutional Law 309(3).
(3) Constitutional Law - Due Process of Law - Civil Remedies and Proceedings - Parties and Process or Notice - Service on Agent of Nonresident.
(4) Lee v. Memphis Publ. Co., 195 Miss. 264, 14 So. 2d 351 (1943).
(5) None.
(6) Constitutional Law -- §§ 929-30.

Questions:

1. Use First Decennial. In a civil case, the postmark on a letter was introduced into evidence. Is the postmark admissible into evidence without proof?

2. Use Second Decennial. Eddie Norton was adjudged an incompetent by of reason habitual drunkenness. Are Eddie's subsequent contracts which affect his property rendered void by this adjudication?

3. Use Third Decennial. A petition was filed with the Minnesota Board of Law Examiners seeking the disbarment of an attorney for alleged misconduct in signing a will as a witness after the testatrix had died. Was the evidence of this alleged misconduct sufficient to sustain the charge?

4. Use Fourth Decennial. Plaintiff sued for rent under a written lease. After finding for the defendant, plaintiff contended that the court lacked jurisdiction since the order had been entered before return to proof of service had been filed. In New Hampshire does failure to file the return deny the court jurisdiction?

5. Use Fifth Decennial. Relying on the Mississippi statute which provided that one was presumed dead if absent for seven years without having been heard from, Freda, whose first husband had been absent and not heard from for more than seven years, married Bill. Subsequent to Freda's marriage to Bill it was discovered that Freda's first husband was alive. Was the marriage of Freda and Bill void?

6. Use Sixth Decennial. Trico Products Corporation sued the Delman Corporation for patent infringement. It appeared that the patents related to an apparatus for discharging liquid onto automobile windshields for cleaning purposes, and were merely the application of mechanical means other than "inventions." The federal trial court rendered judgment for defendant Delman. Under the Federal Rules of

Civil Procedure did the review by the appellate court of the district court's findings and conclusions as to questions of fact result in an affirmance?

7. Use Sixth Decennial. Mr. Lawrence Hawthorne borrowed two sums ($45,000 and $18,000) in 1954 from his partners, Mr. and Mrs. J. M. Walton, and was charged an illegally high interest rate. Mr. Hawthorne repaid the sums and interest, and then sued to recover the excess interest. Has Mr. Hawthorne waived or released his claim of usury by payment?

8. Use Sixth Decennial. Mr. Kinzer was indicted for housebreaking and larceny. The trial ended with a hung jury. During the second trial, Kinzer's counsel moved to subpoena the court reporter from the first trial, for use in cross-examination of government witnesses, after the court denied defendant's request for a free transcript. Disregarding the trial court's denials of defendant's motions, as a general rule will stenographers or reporters notes, taken at a former trial, be dismissed to impeach testimony of witnesses?

9. Use Seventh Decennial. An actress entered into a contract with an agency to be her exclusive representative for a period of five years. Under the contract she was to pay the agency 10% of her earnings. Simultaneously the agency allegedly made an oral agreement to pay 5% of her earnings to another agent to whom she was already under contract. In New York, does the statute of frauds bar enforcement of such an oral agreement made in conjunction with an artist's exclusive agency contract?

10. Use Seventh Decennial. Twice daily a farmer drove his herd of cattle along the main road through a village in Maryland from his barn on one edge of the village to his pasture on the opposite edge. Residents of the village complained that the dropping of manure on the roadway was a nuisance and sought to enjoin the farmer from driving his cattle through the village. In Maryland, does the driving of cattle along a public highway to pasture constitute a nuisance per se?

11. Use Seventh Decennial. Walter J. Borowicz, five years old, was injured in Maplewood, New Jersey, when he was struck by William J. Hood's car. Walter's parents sued Mr. Hood. A policeman, Officer Schuler, testified that he had measured Mr. Hood's skid marks as 63 feet in length. As instructions regarding speed and control of the automobile where injuries resulted from the negligent operation of the vehicle, should the court have instucted the jury as to the skidding?

12. Use Seventh Decennial. Mrs. Geneva Rose and Lawrence Rose, the widow and son, respectively, of the decendent, were sentenced to 10 years for slaying John Rose. Only circumstantial evidence was introduced and that evidence was conflicting. Was this sufficient proof of guilt as to a homicide under criminal law?

13. Use Seventh Decennial. Mr. Gary Mullendore was rear-ended while he was stopped in a line of Kansas City traffic. He sued and won. The

defendant appealed, claiming the trial court erred in giving an instruction allowing the jury to assess damages for mental suffering even though there had been no testimony to that effect. Was defendant's appeal successful?

14. Use Seventh Decennial. At the close of a rather lengthy trial, a jury determined that the decendent's gift three years prior to death had been a valid inter vivos gift, and judgment was rendered in favor of the defendant recipient of the gift. Plaintiff appealed, challenging the jury's finding of fact with respect to intent, delivery, and acceptance. Was the jury's determination allowed to stand on appeal?

15. Use Eighth Decennial. Mr. Louis discovered some heretofore unpublished letters and intended to include those letters in a book. These letters were written by a husband and wife to their children. The children's parents were convicted of treason and ultimately executed. The children attempt to enjoin publication of these letters claiming they are copyrighted. Does the "fair use" doctrine permit use of these materials if it is done in a reasonable manner?

16. Use Eighth Decennial. Sandra and Harry Henry were on a trip across Massachusetts when their car was struck by defendant's vehicle. Sandra was pregnant with viable twin fetuses which were subsequently stillborn. Sandra filed a wrongful death action on behalf of the estates of the two children. Is a stillborn child, a "person" under the Massachusetts Wrongful Death statute?

17. Use Eighth Decennial. A prison inmate was burned over thirty percent of his body when another inmate hurled a "Molotov Cocktail" into his cell. As a result, the inmate was hospitalized for four months, underwent painful skin grafts, and suffered severe nightmares. He was awarded $25,000 for past and future suffering. Were these damages excessive?

18. Use Eighth Decennial. Mary responded to a beauty parlor advertisement for a permanent and wave for only $12.50. The beautician suggested a more expensive and different treatment. Mary agreed. Within a few days her hair became dry and brittle and broke whenever she brushed it. To hide her embarrassment she bought several hair pieces and later took hair treatments to stop her hair from breaking off at the scalp. A jury awarded damages of over $2,000 for her suffering and out of pocket expenses. Was this award reasonable?

19. Use Eighth Decennial. A New York pharmacist advertised through local newspapers discounts on all drug needs and offered free $2.00 certificates for use with all drug purchases. The State Board of Pharmacy charged that this advertising practice was unethical and a violation of a state regulation prohibiting the advertising of discount prescriptions. Was this regulation found to be unconstitutionally vague?

20. Use Eight Decennial. As Joe was proceeding down the highway he was passed by a large tractor trailer truck. Almost immediately the tires of the truck began to smoke and shroud the view of the occupants of the

cars following behind. The truck driver, noticing the smoke, slowly began to reduce his speed and then stopped in the center lane of the highway. Joe crashed into the rear of the truck. Does Joe's action of continuing to drive into the cloud of smoke constitute negligence?

ASSIGNMENT 2
USE OF TABLES TO CONVERT FROM CENTURY DIGEST SECTION NUMBERS TO DECENNIAL DIGEST KEY NUMBERS

Method:

Refer either to Volume 21 of the First Decennial Digest or to Volume 24 of the Second Decennial Digest. Using the table in either location (they're identical), convert the below-listed Century Digest Section Numbers to appropriate Decennial Digest Key Numbers.

Example:

QUESTION: Licences sec. 41
ANSWER: Animals - 4

Questions:

1. Attorney and Client sec. 199
2. Bankruptcy sec. 735
3. Burglary sec. 35
4. Contracts sec. 517
5. Criminal Law sec. 1247
6. Discovery sec. 55
7. Eminent Domain sec. 223
8. Fish sec. 12
9. Guaranty sec. 38
10. Homicide sec. 549
11. Infants sec. 177
12. Landlord and Tenant sec. 567
13. Mortgages sec. 1608
14. Navigable Waters sec. 107
15. Obscenity sec. 16
16. Parent and Child sec. 76
17. Statutes sec. 56

18. Taxation sec. 104

19. Usury sec. 219

20. Wills sec. 1630

ASSIGNMENT 3
USE OF U.S. SUPREME COURT DIGESTS

Method:

Using either the Lawyers Co-operative Publishing Company, U.S. Supreme Court Reports Digest, (Lawyers' Edition) or West's U.S. Supreme Court Digest, answer the problems listed below and provide:

(1) A "Yes" or "No" answer to the question, basing your reply on a relevant digest paragraph.
(2) The "Lawyers' Edition Digest" Topic and Section Number or the "West's U.S. Digest" Topic and Key Number which covers the digest paragraph which answers the question.
(3) The complete citation to the case in point using the latest edition of A Uniform System of Citation for proper form.

Example:

QUESTION: Has the United States Supreme Court spoken about the justification for punishing libels according to Illinois law?

ANSWER:
(1) Yes.
(2) (a) Lawyers' Edition Digest: Libel and Slander §22
(b) West's U.S. Digest: Libel & Slander - 141
(c) Beauharnais v. Illinois, 343 U.S. 250 (1952).

Questions:

1. Does the existence of a statutory right imply the existence of all necessary and appropriate remedies?

2. Does a father have a constitutionally protected right to the custody, care, and management of his children?

3. Can a person other than a citizen take an oath to support the Constitution of the United States?

4. Does the accidental destruction of a house by fire relieve the lessee of liability for rent?

5. An oral confession was used which was made to a doctor at a hospital one hour after the arrest of the defendant who had been shot and had been given two large injections of morphine. Is this in violation of due process?

6. Is evidence by comparison of handwritings admissible when the witness had had no previous knowledge of the writings, but is called

on to testify merely from a comparison?

7. A contract was signed by one of the parties on Sunday, and delivered to an agent of the other party. The assent and signature of the other party were not given until a weekday. Was the contract void, being in violation of a statute making it penal to do any manner of business on Sunday?

8. A testator gave certain real and personal property to a city in trust, forever, for the purpose of building and supporting two colleges. None of the property purchased therefore was to be sold, ever. Is this void as creating a perpetuity?

9. May a witness in federal criminal prosecution be asked leading questions if the inference which will be drawn from the question is factually true?

10. May a state arbitrarily deny admission to practice law?

11. Would a zoning ordinance which is clearly arbitrary and unreasonable and without substantial relation to public health, safety, or general welfare be declared unconstitutional?

12. Is a particular form of words essential to create a trust, provided there is reasonable certainty as to the property, the objects, and the beneficiaries?

13. A statute of state A required all marriages to be entered into in the presence of a magistrate or clergyman and required that the marriage be preceded by a license. The statute was silent as to whether a marriage not complying with its provisions was void. X and Y did not follow this formal procedure but lived together as husband and wife. They claim a common law marriage and that, therefore, their marriage is valid. Are they correct?

14. Does the fact that an alien plaintiff resides in the same state as defendant deprive the federal courts from having jurisdiction over the case?

15. The legislature of state A passed a special act granting X a divorce from Y. Is this divorce valid even though not given by a court of competent jurisdiction?

16. If an attorney had been appointed by the court to represent an accused, must the attorney do so?

17. The public health law of state X provides that any doctor practicing medicine after being convicted of a felony shall be guilty of a misdemeanor. Is this provision valid?

18. X had for many years occupied certain public lands of the U.S. Government. Subsequently, the federal government granted a plot of land to Y. This plot included that land occupied by X. X claims

to have obtained the government's land by adverse possession and that the grant of the land by the government to Y is therefore void. Is this contention correct?

19. A took from B a mortgage on certain real estate containing sandstone quarries which, however, had not been sufficiently worked to determine their extent or value. B, C, and D certified that they had resided in the neighborhood for 20 years and that in their best opinion and judgment the value of the quarry was 150 per cent more than the loan. Upon foreclosure the land brought less than one-sixth the amount of the loan. A sued B, C, and D for damages caused him by their fraud and misrepresentation. Can A recover?

20. The Georgia House of Representatives refused to seat a duly elected representative because of his statements attacking the policy of the Federal Government in Vietnam and the Selective Service laws. Was this refusal unconstitutional based on denial of freedom of speech?

ASSIGNMENT 4
USE OF THE MODERN FEDERAL PRACTICE DIGEST, WEST'S FEDERAL PRACTICE DIGEST, 2d AND WEST'S FEDERAL PRACTICE DIGEST, 3d

Method:

Refer to the Modern Federal Practice Digest, West's Federal Practice Digest, 2d or to West's Federal Practice Digest, 3d. The date the case was decided is given in parenthesis at the end of each problem. In relation to each problem, provide:

(1) A "Yes" or "No" answer to the question contained in the problem.

(2) The Topic and Key Number under which you found the digest paragraph that answered (1), supra.

(3) The complete citation to the case in point using the latest edition of A Uniform System of Citation for proper form.

Example:

QUESTION: Presume that a federal taxpayer has no office, no telephone, no furniture, no seal, and does not hold any meetings. Do these facts establish that the taxpayer is not an association taxable as a corporation?

ANSWER:
(1) No
(2) Internal Revenue - 815
(3) Keating-Snyder Trust v. Commissioner, 126 F.2d 860 (5th Cir. 1942).

1. According to the Nebraska federal trial court, may a public officer charge the person benefited by a service, for additional compensation, absent express statutory authorization? (1946)

2. May the doctrine of res ipsa loquitur be applied under Idaho law in a malpractice action against a physician? (1973)

3. Has any federal court ever passed on the effect to First Amendment rights of free speech concerning the White House restrictions on demonstrations which put a damper on the use of streets and public places for demonstration purposes? (1973)

4. According to the Second Circuit's interpretaiton of 18 U.S.C. § 922(a)(3), is scienter an element of the statute making it unlawful to transport into one's state of residence a firearm or other weapons purchased outside the state? (1973)

5. Does a bank have the right to countermand a traveler's check which it has issued? (1942)

6. Does a purchaser of a cemetery lot acquire a property right which the law recognizes? (1950)

7. Is a lawyer an "officer of the court" within the meaning of the statute empowering courts to punish as contempt misbehavior of its officers in their official transactions? (1956)

8. Under Tennessee law, is a hospital strictly liable for administering a transfusion of blood which is infected with serum hepatitis? (1975)

9. Does the use of force to obtain a legitimate union demand for higher wages evidence the requisite intent for conviction of extortion? (1973)

10. A village passed an ordinance prohibiting the flight of aircraft over the village at an altitude of less than 1,000 feet. Is the ordinance constitutional? (1952)

11. Is proof of conversion to the defendant's use essential to every conviction for embezzlement of CETA funds? (1984)

12. Is a contract of some nature, either express or implied in fact, essential to the right of an attorney to recover for expenses? (1980)

13. May the government break down a single conspiracy into componant subagreements for purpose of multiple punishments or multiple prosecutions? (1977)

14. Does fact that relevant means of knowledge was readily available and open to plaintiff but remained unused preclude liability for willful fraud? (1980)

15. Generally, is there privity between an injured party and the insurer of a wrongdoer? (1984)

16. Is disclosure of a competency report mandated even where the report indicates insanity or incompetency? (1978)

17. Can an ordinance of a municipal corporation which is not overbroad be nevertheless unconstitutional as applied if it is enforced against a protected activity? (1976)

18. Is use of corporal punishment to discipline public school students forbidden simply because it interferes in some instances with the right of parental control? (1976)

19. Does the use of the word "radio" in the Communications Act include television transmission? (1984)

20. Does a statute which makes punishable, inter alia, the receipt of a firearm by an ex-felon infringe on the right to bear arms? (1976)

ASSIGNMENT 5
USE OF THE TABLES OF CASES OF THE AMERICAN DIGEST SYSTEM

Method:

Check the Table of Cases of the appropriate portion of the American Digest System. Locate the following and provide:

(1) The West reporter citation. Do not provide parallel, memo, cert. or rehearing citations.
(2) The first-listed Topic and its first Key Number.

Example:

QUESTION: Heinbach v. Heinbach (1918)
ANSWER: (1) 202 S.W. 1123
(2) Acknowledgement - 54

Questions:

1. Robards v. Rees (1986)
2. Adoptive Parents v. Superior Court in and for Maricopa County (1970)
3. Boies v. Dovico (1965)
4. Cain v. Meade County (1929)
5. State v. Feeler (1982)
6. Daugherty v. Feland (1916)
7. Dorsey v. Petrott (1940)
8. Eustace v. Speckhart (1973)
9. U-Hall Co. v. Liberty Mut. Ins. Co. (1984)
10. Faulk v. Soberanes (1961)
11. Holman v. Oriental Refinery (1965)
12. Ivanhoe Grand Lodge AT & AM of Colo. v. Most Worshipful Grand Lodge of Ancient Free and Accepted Masons of Colo. (1952)
13. Leathers v. Tupelo Coffee Co. (182)
14. Julian v. Harris (1973)
15. King v. Flemming (1961)

16. Levin v. Sohn (1948)

17. Milburn v. McNiff (1985)

18. Perkins v. C.I.R. (1984)

19. Mile High Poultry Farms v. Frazier (1945)

20. Quinlan v. Bussiere (1965)

21. Oregon v. Niles (1985)

22. Southern Seating & Cabinet Co. v. Gladish (1916)

23. BA Leasing Corp. v. Board of Assessment Appeals of State of Colo. (1982)

24. State ex rel Quigg v. Liquidator of Sewer Districts of St. Louis County (1943)

25. Tener v. Hill (1965)

26. Dedek v. Dedek (1984)

27. United States v. Varlack (1955)

28. Velez v. Christian (1973)

29. Flynn, In re Paternity of (1983)

ASSIGNMENT 6
USE OF THE TABLE OF CASES OF THE U.S. SUPREME COURT DIGEST (West Pub. Co.)

Method:

Refer to the Table of Cases of the U.S. Supreme Court Digest (West Pub. Co.) and locate the following cases. For each, provide:

(1) The official (U.S.) citation to the full opinion. Do not provide parallel, memo, cert. or rehearing citations.

(2) The first-listed Topic and Key Number, if any, immediately following the case citation.

Example:

QUESTION: Mills v. Duryee
ANSWER: (1) 11 U.S. (7 Cranch) 481
(2) Debt, Action of - 12

Questions:

1. Aquilino v. United States

2. Buchanan v. City of Litchfield

3. Chemgas v. Tynan

4. De Bary v. Arthur

5. Erskine v. Hohnbach

6. Ex parte Dainard

7. Fisher v. Shropshire

8. Gomillion v. Lightfoot

9. Huff v. Ford

10. In Re Loving

11. International Bank v. Sherman

12. Jeter v. Hewitt

13. The Keokuk

14. Kinsella v. Krueger

15. Leib v. Bolton

16. McKimm v. Riddle
17. Omaha Hotel Co. v. Wade
18. Potts v. Chumasero
19. Quicksall v. Michigan
20. Read v. City of Plattsmouth
21. Sarlls v. United States
22. Scott v. Paisley
23. Town of Mineral Point v. Lee
24. Trbovich v. United Mine Workers of America
25. Urquhart v. Brown
26. United States v. Mosely
27. Villalobos v. United States
28. Willing v. Rinenstock
29. Yee Hem v. United States
30. Zahn v. Board of Public Works of City of Los Angeles

ASSIGNMENT 7
USE OF THE TABLE OF CASES OF THE U.S. SUPREME COURT REPORTS DIGEST, LAWYERS' EDITION

Method:

Refer to the Table of Cases of the U.S. Supreme Court Reports Digest, Lawyers' Edition (Lawyers' Co-op Publ. Co.). Locate the below-listed cases and provide:

(1) The official (U.S.) citation to the full opinion, if any. Do not provide parallel, memo, cert. or rehearing citations.

(2) The first-listed Topic and Section Number, if any, immediately following the case citation.

Example:

QUESTION: Mitchum v. Foster
ANSWER: (1) 407 U.S. 225
(2) Civil Rights §12.5

Questions:

1. The Adeline
2. Bourjois v. Chapman
3. Calder v. Bull
4. Di Piero v. Pennsylvania
5. Ex parte Dainard
6. FHA v. Burr
7. Fisher v. Shropshire
8. Goldsborough v. Orr
9. The Great Republic
10. Jenkins v. McKeithen
11. The Keokuk
12. Kowalski v. Chandler
13. Loving v. Virginia
14. McDonald v. Magruder

15. <u>MacDougall v. Green</u>

16. <u>NLRB v. C & C Plywood Corp.</u>

17. <u>Ohio ex rel. Lloyd v. Dollison</u>

18. <u>Pierce v. Society of the Sisters</u>

19. <u>Quinlan v. Green County</u>

20. <u>Roberts v. Cay</u>

21. <u>Rosenbloom v. Metromedia Inc.</u>

22. <u>Scott v. Paisley</u>

23. <u>Texas & P.R. Co. v. American Tie and Timber Co.</u>

24. <u>Trbovich v. United Mine Workers of America</u>

25. <u>The Umbria</u>

26. <u>Vachon v. New Hampshire</u>

27. <u>Whittington v. Pegelow</u>

28. <u>Wisconsin v. Yoder</u>

29. <u>Yazoo & M. V. R. Co. v. Mullins</u>

30. <u>Zartarian v. Billings</u>

ASSIGNMENT 8
USE OF THE TABLE OF CASES OF WEST'S MODERN FEDERAL PRACTICE DIGEST, FEDERAL PRACTICE DIGEST, 2d AND FEDERAL PRACTICE DIGEST, 3d

Method:

Refer to the Table of Cases of the Modern Federal Practice Digest, the Federal Practice Digest, 2d and the Federal Practice Digest, 3d. Locate the below-listed cases and provide:

(1) The citation for each case. Do not cite reversing, affirming, memo, or cert. cases.

(1) The first-listed Topic and Key Number, if any, immediately following the case citation.

Example:

QUESTION: McGraw-Edition Co. v. Central Transformer Core.
ANSWER: (1) 308F.2d 70 (8th Cir. 1962)
(2) Appeal and Error 198

Questions:

1. The A. H. Quinby (1879)

2. Alexander v. Silverman (1973)

3. Arna v. Northwestern University (1986)

4. Baldwin Rubber Co. v. Paine & Williams Co. (1939)

5. Caraway v. Califano (1980)

6. Carey v. Settle (1966)

7. Dallas Oil & Gas Co., Matter of (1981)

8. In re Chagra (1965)

9. Frankel v. Commissioner of Ed. (1979)

10. Delesdernier v. O'Rourke & Warren Co. (1962)

11. Hayward v. C.I.R. (1984)

12. Ferguson v. Cardwell (1971)

13. G & W Towing Co. v. Barges CB-1 (1966)

14. John Doe Corp. v. Miller (1980)

15. Iannelli v. Long (1971)

16. Meeropol v. Meese (1986)

17. Justh v. Holtman (1965)

18. Lester v. Isbrandtsen Co. (1950)

19. Mack v. 48 Vesey Street Corporation (1947)

20. Samimi v. I.N.S. (1983)

21. NLRB v. Colten (1939)

22. Oy v. Haff (1940)

23. U.C. Castings Co. v. Knight (1985)

24. Petition of Gogate (1942)

25. In re Robertson (1954)

26. W.R. Grace & Co. v. Pullman, Inc. (1976)

27. Rochford v. Volatile (1970)

28. S.S. Audrey J. Luckenbach (1963)

29. U.S. v. Puchi (1971)

30. United States v. Swank (1971)

ASSIGNMENT 9
JUDICIAL DEFINITIONS OF VARIOUS WORDS AND PHRASES

Method:

Using the three indicated sources, locate a judicial definition of the word or phrase stated in the problem. Give only the name of the first case cited, if any, in each source. If none, state "Not Listed."

Sources:
(1) Words and Phrases (W&P)
(2) Federal Practice Digest, 3d, (FPD)
(3) U.S. Supreme Court Digest (West) (WD)

Example:

QUESTION: Fence
ANSWER:
(1) (W&P) Bollenback v. United States
(2) (FPD) Not listed
(3) (WD) Bollenback v. United States

Questions:

1. Abnormal
2. Alien
3. Carrying on Business
4. Contemporaneous
5. De Novo
6. Death
7. Discrimination
8. Easement
9. Employee
10. Entrapment
11. Gratuitous
12. Highest
13. Incorporating
14. Kick-back
15. Lascivious

16. Left
17. Magic Words Doctrine
18. Mens Rea
19. Merger
20. Next of Kin
21. Ordinary Care
22. Outlaw
23. Quorum
24. Refuses to Answer
25. Signature
26. Subrogation
27. Ultra Vires
28. Unusual
29. Waiver
30. X-Rays

ASSIGNMENT 10
THEME AND DRILL PROBLEMS FOR DIGESTS FOR COURT DECISIONS

The problems that follow are designed to acquaint you with the many features and impressive scope of digests. To answer these problems requires analytical thinking on your part. It also often requires you to think like an editor as you try to determine how various words and phrases in an index might provide references to the sources you are researching.

Some hints to help you along the way should make use of the digests almost enjoyable. When the directions ask you to use the most specific digest available, be sure to do so. For example, if the question says it is a U.S. Supreme Court case, use a Supreme Court digest. If it is a federal court case, use a federal digest. If it is a state case, use that state's digest, if available in your library. If the appropriate state digest is unavailable, you must use the decennials or the proper regional digest.

Note also that the problems instruct you to search under a specific Topic and Key Number. Remember that Topics and Key Numbers expand or they are placed under a new Topic in subsequent digests.

Working with the digests provides you with a good opportunity to work on developing proper citation technique through use of A Uniform System of Citation ("Blue Book"). Read about the proper order for citations, parallel citations, and spacing. Place the cases you cite as answers in "Blue Book" form.

THEME PROBLEMS FOR DIGESTS

Theme Problem I:

A. In the West publication of the Brown decision, 74 S. Ct. 686, two Key Numbers under the topic Constitutional Law are assigned in the headnotes. What two numbers are they?

B. Using the Key Numbers in Brown assigned to headnote number four and its subsections as a guide, answer the following questions using the most specific digest your library has available:

1. Locate a 1968 U.S. Supreme Court decision which holds that no official student transfer plan of which racial segregation is the inevitable result can stand under the 14th Amendment.

2. Find a 1970 Federal District Court decision that holds that while no student has a constitutional right to play football, no student can be prohibited from doing so solely on the basis of race.

3. Locate a Federal court of Appeals decision in 1972 that holds that where it is possible to determine whether a school is for whites or blacks simply by reference to the racial composition of its faculty and staff, a prima facie case of violation of Equal Protection is made out.

4. Find a 1936 Maryland case that held that a Negro student was entitled to admission to the law school of the state university where the state could furnish "separate but equal" facilities no other way.

C. Using the Topic and Key Number assigned to headnote number one of Brown as a start, answer the following questions by referring to the most specific digest available in your library.

1. Find a 1977 Georgia case that holds that a county ordinance seeking to regulate "X-rated" movies through special fees, although justified as being merely a business regulation, will be subject to judicial scrutiny.

2. Find a 1974 U.S. Court of Appeals case where a statute forbidding the acceptance of an unlawful gratuity is being invoked against a former U.S. Senator, hypothetical cases showing possible effects on First Amendment should be ignored.

3. Find a 1975 U.S. Court of Appeals decision that holds that where complaining Library of Congress employees have not pointed out certain rules as due process violations, the Court does not have to scrutinize them.

4. Locate a 1942 South Carolina case which holds that where a law condemns a business for protection of public health, the Court will inquire into the law's necessity.

5. Cite a 1977 North Dakota case where a putative father challenging an illegitimacy law who did not assert policies that show the law's unconstitutional application to others will have the Court's inquiry limited to his case.

D. Using the Table of Cases for the most appropriate digest, provide citations for the following cases:

1. Vaughn v. Califano - Federal case. (1977)

2. Zorick v. Jones - Miss. (1966)

3. Aaltio v. Chicago - Minn. (1936)

4. Alford v. Butler - Tenn. (1963)

5. Caldwell v. Sturdivant - Ga. (1923)

Theme Problem II:

A. Roe v. Wade, 93 S. Ct. 705 has one Key Number assigned to headnote 11 and two to headnote 16. List these three Key Numbers.

B. Using the Key Number for headnote 11 and its subsections as a starting place, answer the following questions by referring to the most specific digest available in your library.

1. Find a 1973 Federal District Court case in Connecticut that holds that a statute compelling and unwed mother to appear before a judge, name the putative father and institute a paternity action does not violate the mother's right to privacy.

2. Cite a 1978 N.J. case that affirms that states may impose stricter standards for the protection of individual rights than the Federal Constitution.

3. Find a 1978 Federal case from Texas that holds that the family of an extraordinarily talented high school basketball player had the right to assist the player in developing his talents to the fullest.

4. Cite a 1945 Oklahoma case holding that prohibiting the sale of 3.2 beer in establishments that permit dancing is not violative of state constitutions guarantee of individual rights.

5. Cite a 1967 New Hampshire case that held that a statute forbidding parades on streets and public ways without first obtaining a license did not violate First Amendment guarantees.

C. Using whichever of the Key Numbers attached to headnote 16 (and/or its subdivisions) that seems relevant as a starting place, answer the following:

1. Locate a 1977 case that held invalid a Florida statute that authorized abortions only in certified centers and required doctors to sign a stipulation before each operation.

2. Cite a 1977 Nebraska case that upholds a statute making the possession of one pound or less of marijuana a misdemeanor as not violative of equal protection.

3. Cite a 1975 Federal District Court case in Pennsylvania striking down a Pennsylvania statute that requires a woman to get signed permission from her spouse prior to an abortion.

4. Find a Federal Court of Appeals decision coming from Arizona that holds that failure to make intent a part of the crime of possession of an unregistered firearm does not violate due process.

5. Locate a 1978 Iowa case that finds the undefined term "indecent" as a standard of behavior in a statute to be violative of due process.

D. Using the Table of Cases for the most appropriate digest, provide citations for the following cases:

1. <u>Denneny v. Siegel</u> - Federal case. (1967)

2. <u>Quirici v. Freeman</u> - Cal. (1950)

3. <u>Hoffman v. Victory Rubber Co.</u> - Wash. (1922)

4. <u>Climax Dairy Co. v. Mulder</u> - Colo. (1925)

5. Tresher v. McElroy - Fla. (1925)

DRILL PROBLEMS FOR DIGESTS

Instructions:

A. For each of the hypotheticals in Section A of each Drill Problem Section, use the indicated Decennial Digest and provide:

(1) A "yes" or "no" answer to the question.

(2) The Topic and Key Number under which your answer was found.

(3) The Uniform System of Citation cite form for the case that provides the answer.

NOTE: If you are unable to locate a specific case that yields the "yes" or "no" answer, locate other Topic and Key Numbers that offer cases of interest.

B. In subsection B of each Drill Problem Section, use the case table in the appropriate set of Decennial Digests to complete the citations.

Drill Problem I:

A. Questions:

1. Use Third Decennial. A petition was filed with the Minnesota Board of Law Examiners seeking the disbarment of an attorney for alleged misconduct in signing a will as a witness after the testatrix had died. Was the evidence of this alleged misconduct sufficient to sustain the charge?

2. Use Fourth Decennial. Plaintiff sued for rent under a written lease. After a finding for the defendant, plaintiff contended that the court lacked jurisdiction since the order had been entered before return of proof of service had been filed. In New Hampshire does failure to file the return deny the court jurisdiction?

3. Use Fifth Decennial. Relying on the Mississippi statute which provided that one was presumed dead if absent for seven years without having been heard from, Freda, whose first husband had been absent and not heard from for more than seven years, married Bill. Subsequent to Freda's marriage to Bill it was discovered that Freda's first husband was alive. Was the marriage of Freda and Bill void?

4. Use Sixth Decennial. A San Francisco attorney entered into a contingent fee contract with a client. The contract had the effect of providing additional compensation if a cross-complaint was filed and

successfully defended. Does this make the contract illegal, unfair or inequitable?

5. Use Seventh Decennial. The treasurer of a union local entered into a scheme with the other members of the union's executive board whereby he sold union property and pocketed part of the proceeds. In California does pocketing part of proceeds from sale of realty belonging to union constitute embezzlement?

B. Table of Cases:

1. Dicennials or Regional Digests

   (a) Cain v. Mead County (1929)

   (b) Escobar v. State (1965)

   (c) Groover v. Terrell (1919)

   (d) Idol v. Street (1951)

   (e) Lee County v. James (1937)

2. U.S. Supreme Court Citations

   (a) Chemgas v. Tuyna

   (b) Ghio v. Moore

   (c) Moelle v. Sherwood

   (d) Reaves v. Ainsworth

   (e) Urquhart v. Brown

Drill Problem II:

A. Questions:

1. Use Third Decennial. A city in Arkansas sued to recover possession of a block of land which the city alleged had been dedicated to public use. A plat of the land had been filed in the office of the Recorder of Deeds. The block in question was designated "Franklin Square," but was not put to public use nor ever accepted by the City Council as a public place. Did the marking of the block as a "square" constitute an implied dedication of the land to the city?

2. Use Fourth Decennial. In a suit for specific performance of a contract to sell certain real estate in California, evidence showed that in 1921, the contract was entered into at a purchase price of $3,000, of which $2,853.32 was to be paid in installments. On July 28, 1927, plaintiff tendered $1400 to defendant and demanded that she execute

and deliver a conveyance to him. She refused. In an action for specific performance in the State of California, is tender of money by purchaser, without payment, sufficient to show good faith and diligence?

3. Use Fifth Decennial. A tenant sued his landlord for injuries sustained when he injured his hand on the porcelain handle of a faucet over the kitchen sink in his Chicago apartment. He rented the apartment under a month to month tenancy. The janitor of the building had allegedly promised to repair the faucet, but there was no evidence to show any promise by the landlord to make repairs prior to commencement of the tenancy. Was the landlord liable?

4. Use Sixth Decennial. A woman filed a complaint against an attorney with the Monmouth County, New Jersey, Ethics and Grievance Committee. He retaliated by starting a malicious prosecution action against her. May an attorney predicate a malicious prosecution action on the filing of such a complaint?

5. Use Seventh Decennial. An actress entered into a contract with an agency to be her exclusive representative for a period of five years. Under the contract she was to pay the agency 10% of her earnings. Simultaneously the agency allegedly made an oral agreement to pay 5% of her earnings to another agent to whom she was already under contract. In New York, does the statute of frauds bar enforcement of such an oral agreeement made in conjunction with an artist's exclusive agency contract?

B. Table of Cases:

1. Decennials or Regional Digests:

(a) Carse v. Marsh (1922)

(b) Feyerchak v. Hiatt (1940)

(c) Haggerty v. Clement (1940)

(d) James River Bank v. Hansen (1927)

(e) Locigno v. City of Chicago (1961)

2. U.S. Supreme Court Citations

(a) Ex parte Dainard

(b) Hanna v. Maas

(c) Neil v. Biggers

(d) Scott v. Paisley

(e) Vachon v. New Hampshire

CHAPTER 7

ANNOTATED LAW REPORTS

ASSIGNMENT 1
QUICK INDEX AND INDEX TO ANNOTATIONS: USE OF THE QUICK INDEX AND INDEX TO ANNOTATIONS TO LOCATE ANNOTATIONS ON POINTS OF LAW

Method:

Using the index designated in the following problem sub-sets, locate and cite, using the latest edition of A Uniform System of Citation, annotations on point for each fact situation provided. You may have to refer to the actual annotation in order to provide the year in your citation.

Example:

QUESTION:	A cat as a subject of a larceny.
ANSWER:	Annot., 42 A.L.R.3d 1032 (1972)

Questions:

A. Use the A.L.R. First Series Quick Index to locate the following points of law appearing in A.L.R. 1-175.

1. Right of exclusion from or discrimination against patrons of library.
2. Legality of, and injunction against, peaceful picketing by labor union of plant whose employees are represented by another union as statutory bargaining agent.
3. Coaching law students as ground for disbarment of attorneys.
4. When is an individual deemed an inhabitant of the state within taxing law?
5. The pollution of a stream by mining operations.
6. The liability of a notary public or his bond.
7. Liability of insane person for tort.
8. Irresistible impulse as excuse for crime.
9. Conviction or acquittal of larceny as bar to prosecution for burglary.
10. What constitutes a boarding house.

11. Use of mails for sales of articles having superstitious associations.
12. Correct name of married woman.
13. Civil liability for defamation of the dead.
14. Epilepsy as affecting testamentary capacity.
15. Concealment of pregnancy as ground for annulment of marriage.
16. Assault as ground for disbarment of an attorney.
17. Writings in family bible as documentary evidence.
18. Validity of bequest or trust for care of specified animal.
19. Presence of noxious weeds as ground for rescission of contract for purchase of land.
20. Immoral relations between insured and beneficiary as affecting liability of insurer or interest in proceeds of the policy.

B. Use the A.L.R. Index to Annotations to locate the following points of law appearing in A.L.R.2d 1-100.

1. Juror's inattention from sleepiness as ground for reversal or new trial.
2. Presumption of deliberation or premeditation from the fact of killing.
3. Manifestations of grief by victim or family of victim during criminal trial as ground for reversal, new trial or mistrial.
4. Homicide by fright or shock.
5. Criminal responsibility of husband for rape or assault to commit rape on wife.
6. Public payment of tuition to a sectarian school.
7. Statement of belief as perjury.
8. Discharge for absenteeism as affecting right to unemployment compensation.
9. Identification of accused by his voice.
10. Civil liability of sheriff charged with keeping jail for death or injury to prisoner.
11. Carrier's liability to passenger for injury due to pushing or crowding of passengers therein.

12. Liability of hospital for injury or death in obstetrical cases.
13. Attorney's failure to attend court, or tardiness, as contempt.
14. Malpractice liability with respect to diagnosis and treatment of mental disease.
15. Right of the accused to have defense witnesses free from manacles.
16. Rights in cargoes of wrecked or derelict ships not cast upon the shore.
17. Rights of fraternal society to protection against the use of its name, insignia, or ritual by another organization.
18. Adoption as affecting the right of inheritance through or from natural parent or natural kin.
19. Liability of dentist using force to restrain or discipline patient.
20. Keeping of gasoline on premises as increase of hazard voiding fire insurance policy.

C. Use the A.L.R. Index to Annotations to locate the following points of law appearing in A.L.R.3d 1-100.

1. Claustrophobia as disqualifying juror.
2. Effect of testamentary direction as to disposition of testator's body.
3. Negligence and contributory negligence in suit by rescuer against rescued person.
4. Common-law copyright in the spoken word.
5. Penal offense of sniffing glue or similar volatile intoxicants.
6. Tenants' rights where landlord fails to make repairs, to have them made and set off cost against rent.
7. Free exercise of religion as a defense to prosecution for narcotic offense.
8. Symbols: erection, maintenance, or display of religious structures or symbols on public property as violation of religious freedom.
9. When is a will signed at the "end" or the "foot" as required by statute?
10. Sales of liquor to homosexuals or permitting their congregation at licensed premises as ground for suspension or revocation of liquor license.
11. Attack on judiciary as a whole as indirect contempt.

12. Public disclosure of person's indebtedness as invasion of privacy.

13. Infant's liability for services rendered by attorney under contract with him.

14. Activities of law clerks as illegal practice of law.

15. Prospective or retroactive application of overruling decision.

16. Educational expenses as a deduction for income tax purposes.

17. Literary property in lectures.

18. Hunter's civil liability for unintentionally shooting another person.

19. Validity of statutes making parents liable for torts committed by their minor children.

20. Right of heir's assignee to contest will.

D. Use the A.L.R. Index to Annotations to locate points of law in A.L.R.4th.

1. Privileged communications between accountant and client.

2. Products liability: animal feed or medicines.

3. Homicide as precluding taking under will or intestacy.

4. Sufficiency of access to legal research facilities afforded defendant confined in the state prison or local jail.

5. Civil liability for insulting or abusive language -- modern status.

6. Regulation of the practice of acupuncture.

7. Right of jailed or imprisoned parent to visit from minor child.

8. Attorney's failure to attent court, or tardiness, as contempt.

9. Admissibility of hearsay evidence in probation revocation hearings.

10. Liability for negligent operation of dune buggy.

11. Odor of narcotics as providing probable cause for warrantless search.

12. Fact that witness undergoes hypnotic examination as affecting admissibility of testimony in civil case.

13. Modern trends as to tort liability of child of tender years.

14. Recovery by bank of money paid out to customer by mistake.

15. Disclosure or use of computer application software as misappropriation of trade secret.

E. Use the A.L.R. Index to Annotations to locate the following points of law appearing in A.L.R. Fed.

1. Inability of employer to pay wages and damages as defense to wage order under Fair Labor Standards Act.

2. Authority of Secretary of Army to deny dredging and filling permit for ecological reasons under Sec. 10 of Rivers and Harbors Act of 1899.

3. Making, selling or distributing counterfeit tape recordings as violation of federal law.

4. Liability of the United States under Federal Tort Claims Act for damages caused by ingestion or administration of drugs and vaccines approved as safe for use by government agency.

5. Right of accused to bill of particulars in criminal prosecution for evasion of federal income taxes.

6. Acquittal or conviction in state court as bar to federal prosecution based on same fact.

7. Right of accused to inspect the minutes of federal grand jury.

8. Application in federal civil action of governmental privilege of nondisclosure of identity of informer.

9. Construction and application of Food Stamp Act of 1964 establishing food stamp program.

10. Discharge from Armed Forces on ground of conscientious objection.

11. Validity and construction of federal statute requiring registration on crossing border of narcotics user.

12. Unauthorized photocopying by library as infringement of copyright.

13. What acts amount to violation of Hatch Political Activities Act provisions against political activities of certain state and local employees?

14. Construction and application of provision of Freedom of Information Act exempting from disclosure personnel and medical files.

15. Sex discrimination in athletics, validity under federal law.

ASSIGNMENT 2
USE OF TABLE OF CASES OF A.L.R. DIGESTS TO LOCATE CASE CITATIONS AND ANNOTATIONS

Method:

For the following problem sub-sets, refer to the Table of Cases of the Permanent A.L.R. Digest and the A.L.R.2d Digest. Provide the case citation and the cite to the A.L.R. annotation, omitting dates.

Example:

QUESTION: Dunn v. White
ANSWER: 206 Kan. 278, 479 P.2d 215, 47 A.L.R.3d 1289

Questions:

A. Use the Permanent A.L.R. Digest (covering A.L.R. vols. 1-175) Table of Cases.

1. Henson v. Henson
2. Keith v. Kilmer
3. Markovitz v. Markovitz
4. Shulkin v. Shulkin
5. Ziehm v. Vale
6. Crabtree v. Crabtree
7. Brown v. Brown

B. Use the A.L.R.2d 1-100 Digest, Table of Cases Volume.

8. Johnson v. Johnson
9. Kennedy v. Parrott
10. Agnew v. American Ice Co.
11. Coolidge & Sickler Inc. v. Regn
12. Wilson v. Anderson
13. Cleveland v. Detroit
14. McKinley v. Long
15. Jackson v. Jackson

ASSIGNMENT 3
A.L.R. INDEX TO ANNOTATIONS: USE OF THE A.L.R. INDEX TO ANNOTATIONS TO LOCATE ANNOTATIONS FROM AMERICAN LAW REPORTS (1ST, 2D, 3D, 4TH AND FED.) AND LAWYERS EDITION (1ST AND 2D)

Method:

Refer to the A.L.R. Index to Annotations. Find the Annotation History Table. For each of the following annotations cite any supplementing or superseding annotation. Do not consult the pocket part.

Example:

QUESTION: 2 A.L.R. 1376
ANSWER: Superseded 45 A.L.R.2d 1296

Questions:

1. 3 A.L.R. 1130
2. 20 A.L.R. 407
3. 29 A.L.R. 140
4. 18 A.L.R. 197
5. 17 A.L.R. 760
6. 92 A.L.R.2d 421
7. 42 A.L.R.3d 560
8. 75 A.L.R.3d 1000
9. 132 A.L.R. 191
10. 129 A.L.R. 751
11. 90 A.L.R. 1377
12. 22 A.L.R.2d 427
13. 132 A.L.R. 679
14. 118 A.L.R. 1357
15. 97 A.L.R. 1197

ASSIGNMENT 4
USE OF THE A.L.R.2D DIGEST TO LOCATE CASES THAT HAVE BEEN ADDED TO ANNOTATIONS

Method:

Refer to the A.L.R.2d Digest for each of the following fact situations and cite the case name and the A.L.R.2d Annotation reference that follows the case name.

Example:

QUESTION: Bobby Nissan is present when Jay Myron threatens and strikes Roy Martin. Nissan shouts encouragement to Myron to strike Martin again, which Myron does. Martin sues Nissan for the tort of assault and battery.

ANSWER: Hargis v. Horine, 72 A.L.R.2d 1223

Questions:

1. Pedro Montez holds commerical "cockfights" or contests between two roosters armed with artificial spurs. Pedro is arrested and charged with cruelty to animals. He contends that cockfighting is a lawful sport.

2. Charlie Speedo fails to stop after the car he is driving strikes a dog. As a matter of law does his action constitute breach of the peace?

3. Donald Durham, a property owner, shoots and kills a trespassing dog. Does he incur civil liability to the owner of the dog?

4. The proprietor of a golf course offers a prize of $5,000 to any member of the public who shoots a hole in one on his golf course and pays $1 for the opportunity. Fred Fortune pays his dollar and shoots a hole in one. The golf course proprietor refuses to pay the $5,000 contending that the contract was invalid as a "gambling" contract.

5. Rosie Reed promises to give her unborn illegitimate child the given name of the putative father in return for his promise to support the child. Is Rosie's promise adequate consideration for a binding contract?

6. Police Officer Robert Rood arrests and imprisons Larry Lane under a mistaken belief that his is the man named in the warrant. Lane sues Rood for false arrest and unlawful imprisonment. Rood alleges as his defense, the lack of malice or improper motive in making the arrest.

7. Charlie Low beats and pursues his wife to a river bank. He tells her

to jump or he will push her. Charlie knows she cannot swim and the river is deep. She jumps and drowns. Charlie makes no effort to help her or summon assistance. He is charged with homicide.

8. Alice and Roger, although living apart because of Roger's heavy drinking, were still married at the time of Alice's death. Eric Eager, a mortician, furnishes Alice with the usual funeral. He seeks payment from Roger, who refuses to pay, contending that his liability for the necessaries of his wife ended upon her death.

9. Adolph Sparks seeks to pay his hospitalization insurance premium on the Monday immediately following the last day of his grace period (Sunday). The insurance company cancels his policy and he sues to reinstate the policy.

10. Noe Nardi, a member of an unincorporated labor union, requests to inspect its financial records. The union refuses his request and Nardi seeks a court order.

11. Elsie Dinsmore is the beneficiary of a testamentary trust which stipulates that the entire corpus will be turned over to her at the age of 32 providing that she has not married a Catholic. She challenges this provision in court as contrary to public policy and therefore void.

12. Paul Pope, a pedestrian, is severely injured by the breaking of a plate glass window in the Arista Department Store during a windstorm. Arista denies that its negligence was the proximate cause of the injury, citing the gusty wind as a superseding cause.

13. Willie Hinkle, a burglar, was hurrying home with his loot of cash and jewels when Salty Macha waved a revolver in front of him and said, "This is a stick-up. Give me your money and jewelry." Willie handed over everything he had stolen to Salty. Salty was later apprehended and at his trial for robbery contends that the proceeds of a burglary cannot be the subject of a robbery.

14. Nuns of a Roman Catholic order teach in a public school wearing distinctive religious garb. A local organization seeks a court order to comple them to wear normal lay clothing while engaged in teaching.

15. Herman Yellin is a school teacher who is in arrears in the payment of debt to the Friendly Finance Company. Friendly Finance writes to Yellin's school superintendent stating that Yellin owes them money, that normal collection efforts have failed, and seeks advice as to whether Yellin is able to pay, before taking further action. Yellin sues for libel. Friendly Finance alleges Yellin states no cause of action without a plea of special damage.

16. Susan Bee is severely injured by the negligent driving of Allen Alfa. Susan's minor son Daniel sues Alfa for loss of his mother's care and attention. Alfa denies Daniel Bee has a cause of action.

17. Robert and Marcia marry. Shortly thereafter Robert learns that Marcia had sexual intercourse with other men prior to their marriage. Robert seeks an annulment of their marriage alleging fraud on the part of Marcia in not divulging her previous incontinence to him.

18. Dr. Hall, in the act of removing sutures from the toe of Jane Fern, a 4 year old patient, strikes her to make her lie still. A bruise remains sore for some weeks. Her father brings an action for assault and battery against Dr. Hall on her behalf.

19. John Brown, a farmer, seeing some boys in the act of stealing watermelons from his fields, fires his rifle to frighten them off. He fires toward a wooded area where unknown to him another boy is hiding. The other boy is severely injured and an action is brought against Brown for assault and battery. Brown claims he is not civilly liable as he acted in defense of his property and he did not intend to injure the boy.

20. Peter Glass, an attorney, is convicted of willful evasion of federal income taxes, a felony. He is disbarred for conviction of an offense involving fraud or moral turpitude. He contends that income tax evasion is not an offense involving fraud or moral turpitude, and that disbarment as opposed to a suspension was excessive.

ASSIGNMENT 5
A.L.R. DIGESTS: USE OF THE A.L.R. DIGESTS TO LOCATE ANNOTATIONS ON POINTS OF LAW APPEARING IN A.L.R. 2D, 3D, 4TH AND FEDERAL

Method:

For questions 1-10, refer to A.L.R.2d Digest. For questions 11-26, refer to A.L.R. Digest to 3d, 4th and Federal. Locate and cite, in proper form, the A.L.R.2d annotation on each of the following points of law.

Example:

QUESTION: Due process of law as violated by statute or ordinance providing for destruction of dogs without notice or hearing.
ANSWER: Annot., 56 A.L.R.2d 1037 (1957)

Questions:

1. Failure of artisan or construction contractor to procure occupational or business license or permit as affecting validity of contract.

2. Civil liability for use of firearm in defense of habitation or property.

3. Landlord's duty under express covenant to rebuild or restore, where property is damaged or destroyed by fire.

4. Fact that gun was unloaded as affecting criminal responsibility.

5. Right of owner of housing development or apartment houses to restrict canvassing, peddling, solicitations of contributions, etc.

6. Alteration of figures indicating amount of check, bill or note without change in written words as forgery.

7. Liability for statement or publication representing plaintiff as cruel to or killer of animals.

8. Truant or attendance officer's liability for assault and battery.

9. Criminal responsibility of husband for rape, or assault to commit rape on wife.

10. Character and duration of tenancy created by entry under invalid or unenforceable lease.

Chapter 7

Method:

Refer to A.L.R. Digest to 3d, 4th and Federal. Locate and cite, in proper form, the A.L.R. 3d, 4th or Federal annotation on each of the following points of law.

11. Sex discrimination in the United States Armed Forces.

12. Amount of attorneys' fees in matters involving domestic relations.

13. Insulting words addressed directly to police officer as breach of peace or disorderly conduct.

14. Expenses for which condominium association may assess unit owners.

15. Increase in tuition as actionable in suit by student against college or university.

16. Liability in damages for withholding corpse from relatives.

17. Embezzlement, larceny, false pretenses, or allied criminal fraud by partner.

18. Power of court to remove or suspend judge.

19. Validity, construction, and effect of "Sunday closing" or "blue" laws --modern status.

20. Criminal liability for wrongfully obtaining unemployment benefits.

21. What constitutes "property" obtained within extortion statute.

22. Meaning of the term "hotel" as used in zoning ordinance.

23. Interference with radio or television reception as nuisance.

24. Court-authorized permanent or temporary removal of child by parent to foreign country.

25. Picketing court or judge as contempt.

ASSIGNMENT 6
A.L.R.2D LATER CASE SERVICE:
USE OF A.L.R.2D, LATER CASE SERVICE TO LOCATE RELEVANT DECISIONS APPEARING SUBSEQUENT TO ANNOTATIONS PUBLISHED IN A.L.R.2D

Method:

Refer to A.L.R.2d, Later Case Service. For each of the following annotations give the name and citation, according to the latest edition of A Uniform System of Citation, of the described subsequent case. You may have to refer to the actual case you located in order to provide the complete citation.

Example:

QUESTION: 14 A.L.R.2d 7.
Subsequent common-law marriage does not raise presumption that former marriage terminated in divorce.

ANSWER: Lumbermans Mut. Cas. Co. v. Reed, 84 Ga. App. 541, 66 S.E.2d 360 (1951).

Questions:

1. 5 A.L.R.2d 874.
Trial court properly awarded counsel fees to city where taxpayer's case so clearly lacked merit that public interest was not clearly vindicated or served by such litigation.

2. 5 A.L.R.2d 1143.
Under common law, where offense occurred February 25, 1967 at 4:30 P.M. and defendant was born February 25, 1950 at 6:32 P.M., defendant had reached 17 years of age at time of offense.

3. 6 A.L.R.2d 859.
Allegations that divorced wife used alimony payments for alcohol and drugs and had been arrested 50 or more times and confined in jail on many of these occasions did not justify modification of decree for alimony, at least in absence of allegation on part of divorced husband of inability to continue payments or lack of need on part of wife.

4. 64 A.L.R.2d 100.
Recovery was allowed for subsequent illness resulting from plaintiff discovering unpackaged prophylactic in remaining contents of bottle of Coca-Cola after having drunk a portion thereof.

5. 64 A.L.R.2d 301.
Misconduct while practicing law in another state which included among other things borrowing and failing to return books from the county law library warranted denial of admission to bar.

6. 64 A.L.R.2d 600.
Where spectator at pretrial hearing in Black panther criminal

prosecution disrupted proceeding and was summarily adjudged guilty of contempt, judge was not required to refer contempt proceeding to another judge.

7. 78 A.L.R.2d 905.
Results of breathalyzer test were properly suppressed where officer failed to advise defendant of his right to have additional tests administered by any qualified person of his choosing.

8. 7 A.L.R.2d 8.
Presumption of gratuity need not apply where adult or emancipated child, by prearrangement with parent, gives up established home and moves into home of parent, not for purpose of reestablishing family relationship, but for purpose of rendering services of an extraordinarily burdensome nature over long period of time.

9. 22 A.L.R.2d 244.
Alien who admitted homosexual practices with 6 women was not of good moral character as the ordinary man or woman sees it.

10. 24 A.L.R.2d 873.
Acts of cruelty occurring after his wife became insane could not be relied upon by husband as ground for divorce.

11. 24 A.L.R.2d 1288.
Where client's mental incompetence was well-known to attorney, it was his duty to insist that she procure independent advice before deeding her home to him, and his failure to do so rendered the deed void.

12. 25 A.L.R.2d 315.
Discharge of waitresses who walked off job in protest against discharge of friendly supervisor was not unfair labor practice.

13. 27 A.L.R.2d 498.
Congress never intended dependency exemption to be construed so literally as to allow exemption for individual whom taxpayer maintains in an illicit relationship in violation of criminal law of state.

14. 37 A.L.R.2d 551.
Cost of trip to Lourdes shrine in hope of physical improvement not deductible as medical expense.

15. 91 A.L.R.2d 1120.
Claim that juror stated that decision was based upon racial prejudice because defendant was Negro and "that all those people had Cadillacs" was not ground for new trial where there was no showing that any statement by a juror as to race influenced any other juror.

ASSIGNMENT 7
A.L.R. BLUE BOOK OF SUPPLEMENTAL DECISIONS: USE OF THE A.L.R. BLUE BOOK OF SUPPLEMENTAL DECISIONS TO LOCATE LATER DECISIONS AND ANNOTATIONS SUPPLEMENTING OR SUPERSEDING ANNOTATIONS PUBLISHED IN A.L.R. FIRST SERIES

Method:

Refer to the A.L.R. Blue Book of Supplemental Decisions bound volumes 1-5 only. Give the full case name and citation according to the latest edition of A Uniform System of Citation of the first case appearing there subsequent to the publication of each of the following annotations (one case only). Cite all supplementing annotations and any superseding annotation.

Example:

QUESTION: 83 A.L.R. 127.
ANSWER: Davis v. Mississippi, 394 U.S. 721 (1969).
Division III superseded 46 A.L.R.3d 900.

Questions:

1. 3 A.L.R. 1682.
2. 56 A.L.R. 666.
3. 23 A.L.R. 1402.
4. 46 A.L.R. 792.
5. 79 A.L.R. 688.
6. 100 A.L.R. 814.
7. 109 A.L.R. 892.
8. 109 A.L.R. 1148.
9. 133 A.L.R. 11.
10. 70 A.L.R. 817.
11. 10 A.L.R. 1137.
12. 58 A.L.R. 737.
13. 66 A.L.R. 439.
14. 77 A.L.R. 1165.
15. 78 A.L.R. 766.

ASSIGNMENT 8
POCKET SUPPLEMENTS:
USE OF A.L.R.3D POCKET SUPPLEMENTS TO LOCATE RELEVANT DECISIONS SUBSEQUENT TO ANNOTATIONS PUBLISHED IN A.L.R.3D

Method:

Refer to the pocket part in the appropriate volume of A.L.R.3d for each of the following annotations. Give the name and citation, according to the latest edition of A Uniform System of Citation, of the described subsequent case. You may have to refer to the actual case in order to obtain necessary information for the complete citation.

Example:

QUESTION: 92 A.L.R.3d 545
Testimony as to assault by defendant upon woman occurring 75 feet from where body of victim in homicide prosecution was found, in remote area, was properly admitted against defendant, even though assault occurred two years after homicide.

ANSWER: State v. Ellis, 208 Neb. 379, 303 N.W.2d 741 (1981).

Questions:

1. 11 A.L.R.3d 907.
Where an attorney living in one state gave legal advice to his sister living in another state in which he was not admitted, recovery in suit for fee was not barred.

2. 3 A.L.R.3d 829.
Law school expenses incurred by taxpayer to maintain and improve skills as forensic pathologist held deductible.

3. 1 A.L.R.3d 849.
Calling rabbi a "crook" was not actionable per se.

4. 7 A.L.R.3d 1040.
Finding that juror took one drink with her lunch during noon recess was insufficient to require setting aside conviction of defendant where nothing in record reflected incapacity of juror to perform her duties.

5. 14 A.L.R.3d 1201.
High school student's suspension for wearing Confederate flag on jacket did not violate First and Fourteenth Amendments.

6. 14 A.L.R.3d 993.
Promoter of wrestling match held not liable for injuries to patron from being inadvertently bumped by policeman while expelling another patron.

7. 6 A.L.R.3d 1446.
Attorney who split legal fees for referrals from person supposedly a member of the bar in Cuba, but not a member of bar in any state in the U.S., was in violation of Code of Professional Responsibility.

8. 21 A.L.R.3d 116.
In prosecution for murder by running over deceased with automobile, conviction was sustained where evidence showed that accused intended to kill two other persons at time of act, although there was little or no evidence that he intended to kill the deceased.

9. 21 A.L.R.3d 603.
Owner of wild animal (a chimpanzee) was liable to one injured by animal under strict or absolute liability doctrine.

10. 21 A.L.R.3d 641.
Operating boarding house for mentally retarded persons for financial consideration as violation of covenant restricting use to residential purposes.

11. 27 A.L.R.3d 1274.
Surgeon's action in performing operation upon wrong person, while admittedly negligent, did not warrant award of punitive damages where surgeon did not know that he was operating upon wrong patient.

12. 27 A.L.R.3d 794.
If one who was beneficiary under insurance policies upon lives of his wife and daughter was insane when he killed them, he would be entitled to proceeds.

13. 17 A.L.R.3d 1442.
In malpractice action alleging that attorney failed to file personal injury action within the statute of limitations period, expert testimony as to reasonable settlement value or verdict value was inadmissable.

14. 38 A.L.R. 3d 419.
Although square dancer might have assumed risks inherent in square dancing, such as being kicked by another dancer, she did not assume risk of faulty and dangerous floor.

15. 40 A.L.R.3d 444.
Word "child" as used in statute means unborn child whose heart is beating, who is experiencing electronically measurable brainwaves, who is discernably moving, and who is so far developed as to be capable of surviving trauma of birth with aid of usual medical facilities.

ASSIGNMENT 9
POCKET SUPPLEMENTS:
USE OF POCKET SUPPLEMENTS (POCKET PARTS) TO A.L.R.3D, A.L.R. 4TH, AND A.L.R. FED. TO LOCATE LATER CASES THAT SUPPLEMENT THE ANNOTATION.

Method:

Refer to the pocket supplement of the appropriate volume of A.L.R.3d, A.L.R.4th or A.L.R. Federal and provide the name of the first case that supplements the A.L.R. volume and section number in the following problems.

Example:

QUESTION: 2 A.L.R. Fed. 18 §9(a)
ANSWER: Andrews v. Maher

Questions:

1. 2 A.L.R. Fed. 376 §6(e)

2. 1 A.L.R.4th 411 §2(b)

3. 50 A.L.R.3d 1311 §9(a)

4. 2 A.L.R.4th 27 §8(g)

5. 13 A.L.R. Fed. 145 §2(b)

6. 8 A.L.R.4th 70 §3(b)

7. 42 A.L.R.3d §6(a)

8. 13 A.L.R.4th §5

9. 3 A.L.R.3d §4(b)

10. 20 A.L.R.4th §4

11. 18 A.L.R.4th 249 §7

12. 23 A.L.R. Fed. 895 §4(a)

13. 15 A.L.R.4th 294 §6(a)

14. 4 A.L.R. Fed. 123 §18(a)

15. 68 A.L.R.3d 7 §6(a)

ASSIGNMENT 10
A.L.R. TABLE OF LAWS, RULES AND REGULATIONS: USE OF THE TABLE OF LAWS, RULES, AND REGULATIONS IN THE INDEX ANNOTATIONS TO LOCATE STATUTES AND REGULATIONS IN A.L.R. FEDERAL

Method:

Refer to the A.L.R. Table of Laws, Rules and Regulations in the Index to Annotations. Give the first listed citation to a place in A.L.R. Federal where the following federal laws or regulations are cited.

Example:

QUESTION: 42 C.F.R. 203
ANSWER: 71 A.L.R. Fed. 961

Questions:

1. 5 U.S.C.S. sec. 102
2. 7 U.S.C.S. sec. 612
3. 8 U.S.C.S. sec. 1152
4. 8 U.S.C.S. sec. 1329
5. 10 U.S.C.S. sec. 802
6. 5 C.F.R. sec. 151.122
7. 7 C.F.R. sec. 1.51
8. 7 C.F.R. sec. 273
9. 10 C.F.R. sec. 211.67
10. 20 C.F.R. sec. 3.4
11. 22 U.S.C.S. sec. 1203
12. 33 U.S.C.S. sec. 1367
13. 35 U.S.C.S. sec. 23
14. 39 U.S.C.S. sec. 201
15. 40 U.S.C.S. sec. 258
16. Rule 30 (Fed. Rules of Civil Procedure)
17. Rule 36 (Fed. Rules of Civil Procedure)

Chapter 7

18. Rule 59 (Fed. Rules of Civil Procedure)

19. Rule 26 (Fed. Rules of Criminal Procedure)

20. Rule 27 (Rules of U.S. Supreme Court)

ASSIGNMENT 11
WORDS AND PHRASES:
USE OF A.L.R. DIGEST AND BLUE BOOK OF SUPPLEMENTAL DECISIONS TO LOCATE DEFINITIONS OF WORDS AND PHRASES

Method:

Refer to the Words and Phrases Section of the A.L.R. Digest and A.L.R. Blue Book of Supplemental Decisions to locate definitions or annotations on point for the questions in each subset below.

Example:

QUESTION: Declaration
ANSWER: 60 A.L.R.2d 124

Questions:

Using the A.L.R. Digest, A.L.R. Blue Book of Supplemental Decisions, Permanent vols. 4 (1959-67) and 6 (1976-1983) and cite an A.L.R. annotation on point for each of the following words appearing under "Words and Phrases." Include in your answer any supplementing or superseding annotations which have appeared in A.L.R. or A.L.R.2d.

1. Poor person
2. Endangering life
3. Nepotism
4. Warranty
5. Successful parties
6. Accord and satisfaction
7. Accession
8. Action for the recovery of money only
9. Actual doubt
10. "As is"
11. Barratry
12. Blood relations
13. Born out of wedlock
14. Death by own hand

15. Duration of war
16. Double derivative suits
17. End of war
18. Habitual drunkenness
19. Lobbying
20. Member of a family
21. Natural flow
22. Real estate board
23. Slot machine
24. Severance pay
25. Standing timber

ASSIGNMENT 12
THEME AND DRILL PROBLEMS

Theme Problem I:

A. Using the A.L.R. Index to Annotations and A.L.R. volumes, answer the following:

1. Give the title and citation of an A.L.R. annotation on the defacto segregation of the races in public schools.

2. On what case is the annotation based?

3. Where are open enrollment plans discussed?

4. Cite a related law review article by Fiss.

5. In what section can a California case be found?

6. Cite a federal case from Texas that comments on §2(b).

7. Has this annotation been superseded or supplemented?

8. Where might one look in Am. Jur. 2d for a related discussion?

9. Where can one find an A.L.R.2d Comment-Note on Racial Segregation?

10. Where is Brown cited in this annotation?

B. Using the same volume of A.L.R.3d, answer the following:

1. Give the name and citation of an annotation that discusses marriage or pregnancy of a public school student as grounds for expulsion or exclusion, or of restriction of activity.

2. In what section is there discussion of situations where exclusion and expulsion have been upheld?

3. What earlier annotation does this annotation supersede?

4. On what case is this annotation based?

5. Where could one find a related annotation on the application of state law to sex discrimination in sports?

6. Who wrote the briefs of counsel for appellant?

C. Using the same volume, give the citations for the following cases:

1. McCrossen v. United States

2. <u>Yarrington v. Thornburg</u>

3. <u>Russell v. Casebolt</u>

<u>Theme Problem II</u>:

A. Using the A.L.R. Index to Annotations and A.L.R. volumes, answer the following questions:

1. Give the title and citation of an annotation dealing with the right of a woman to have an abortion against the wishes of the child's father.

2. What case is the annotation based on?

3. Has the annotation been superseded or supplemented?

4. In the same volume, find an annotation that discusses what constitutes a church for purpose of worship.

B. Using the annotation found in A.4 answer the following:

1. Where would the issue of whether the home of a priest should be considered as part of the Church be discussed?

2. Where are Wisconsin cases discussed?

3. What treatise is suggested as a reference?

4. Where in Am. Jur. 2d is the same topic discussed?

5. What case is it based on?

C. Using the same volume, give full citations for each of the following cases:

1. <u>Ventress v. Rice</u>

2. <u>Grinnell v. Sard</u>

3. <u>State v. Bagenehl</u>

D. Using the same volume, answer the following:

1. Cite an annotation, including the title, dealing with damages caused by dredging.

2. Cite an annotation, including the title, dealing with the conviction of narcotics offenders due to unlawful entrapment.

Chapter 7

Drill Problem I:

A. Turn to 69 A.L.R.3d 845 (1976) and answer the following:

1. What sections of this annotation cite Louisiana cases?

2. Where could one find discussion of the incapacity of a plaintiff to sue?

3. Where in Am. Jur. 2d could you find a related discussion?

4. On what case is this annotation based?

5. Are there any new cases on §6 since the annotation was published?

6. Where could one find a related annotation on the power of a court to vacate or modify an order granting a new trial in a civil case?

B. Locate annotations on the following topics:

1. The validity of traffic regulations requiring motorcyclists to wear protective headgear.

2. The attempt to commit assault as a criminal offense.

3. The liability of Roy Rogers if Trigger kicks someone.

C. Specify any annotations that supplement or supersede any of the following:

1. 25 A.L.R.2d 1077

2. 41 A.L.R. 1437

3. 75 A.L.R.3d 1000

D. Use the A.L.R. Blue Books (Permanent Edition and Supplements) to answer the following:

1. Cite a case in 379 N.Y.S.2d that updates 90 A.L.R. 101-116.

2. Is there a 1977 Louisiana decision related to 52 A.L.R. 935-341? If so, give citation.

E. Use the A.L.R.2d Later Case Service to answer the following:

1. Cite a case updating 12 A.L.R.2d 524-573, §10 that involves beer barrels.

2. Cite a Pennsylvania case in 227 Pa. Super. that updates §26 of 55 A.L.R.2d 554-63A.

F. Use the pocket parts of A.L.R.3d and A.L.R. Fed. to answer the following:

1. Cite a Conn. case that updated §25 of 72 A.L.R.3d 131-329.

2. Cite an Arizona case that updates §10 of 67 A.L.R.3d 824-889.

3. Cite two Am. Jur. 2d sections that discuss 31 A.L.R.3d 1448-1454.

Drill Problem II:

A. Turn to 84 A.L.R.3d 665 and answer the following:

1. Where in this annotation can one find discussion of the waiving of a guardian's consent?

2. Where in Am. Jur. 2d could one find a discussion of the same topic?

3. Where are any Oklahoma cases cited?

4. Where could one find related discussion on the adoption of an adult?

5. On what case is this annotation based?

B. Locate annotations on the following topics:

1. Statutes related to sexual psychopaths.

2. Exemption from taxation of a municipally owned auditorium.

3. The application of zoning ordinances to a research laboratory.

C. Specify any annotations that supplement or supersede any of the following:

1. 163 A.L.R. 1188

2. 153 A.L.R. 329

3. 1 A.L.R. 148

D. Use the A.L.R. Blue Books (Permanent Edition and Supplements) to answer the following:

1. Cite a case in 324 N.E.2d that cites to the annotation at 10 A.L.R. 1591-1594.

2. What is the latest information on 15 A.L.R. 125-145?

E. Use the A.L.R.2d Later Case Service to answer the following:

1. Cite a Conn. case updating §3 of 15 A.L.R.2d 11-94.

2. Cite a Washington case that updates §39(b) of 70 A.L.R.2d 268-335.

F. Use the pocket parts of A.L.R.3d and A.L.R. Fed. to answer the following:

1. Cite a 5th Circuit case from Texas that updates §3 of 14 A.L.R. Fed. 806-818.

2. Cite an Am. Jur. Proof of Facts 2d article on §1, 60 A.L.R.3d, 880-923.

3. Cite a 6th Circuit decision updating §6, 3 A.L.R. Fed. 569-586.

CHAPTER 8

CONSTITUTIONS

ASSIGNMENT 1
UNITED STATES CONSTITUTION

Sources: United States Code Annotated (Constitution of the United States Annotated)

United States Code Service (Constitution volumes)

The Constitution of the United States of America (Library of Congress, 1987)

Method:

Briefly answer the questions, using one of the above source materials. List the applicable article, section, and clause of the Constitution, and if the question involves judicial interpretation of a constitutional provision, cite a case in point.

Questions:

1. The City of Burbank sought enforcement of its city ordinance prohibiting take-off by jet aircraft from an airport between the hours of 11:00 p.m. and 7:00 a.m. Lockheed Air Terminal, Inc. resisted. What result? (Use Constitution of the United States of America.)

2. Is a member of Congress eligible to hold a commission in the Armed Forces during his continuance in office as a Congressman? (Use Constitution of the United of America or U.S.C.S. or U.S.C.A.)

3. What House of Congress has the sole power to try all impeachments? (Use Constitution of the United States of America or U.S.C.S or U.S.C.A.)

4. What vote is required for a House of Congress to expel a member? (Use Constitution of the United States of America or U.S.C.S. or U.S.C.A.)

5. If the President vetoes a bill and returns it to the House of Congress in which it originated, what formalities are necessary to overrride the veto and make the bill a law? (Use Constitution of the United States of America or U.S.C.S. or U.S.C.A.)

6. For what Federal officials must the President have the advise and consent of the Senate to effect their appointment to Federal office? (Use Constitution of the United States of America or U.S.C.S. or U.S.C.A.)

7. What limitations does the Constitution provide as to the formation of new States of the Union? (Use Constitution of the United States of America or U.S.C.S. or U.S.C.A.)

8. What constitutional provision regulates interstate compacts? (Use Constitution of the United States of America or U.S.C.S. or U.S.C.A.)

9. Are treaties the supreme law of the land? (Use Constitution of the United States of America or U.S.C.S. or U.S.C.A.)

10. If a Vice President assumes the office of President in the first year of his predecessor's elected term, may he seek reelection on his own a second time? (Use Constitution of the United States of America or U.S.C.S. or U.S.C.A.)

11. Under what constitutional authority does the Supreme Court act in reviewing the judgments and decrees of the supreme courts of the several states when federal questions are involved? (Use Constitution of the United States of America or U.S.C.S. or U.S.C.A.)

12. Does Congress have power to impose higher taxes in one state than in another? (Use Constitution of the United States of America or U.S.C.S. or U.S.C.A.)

13. For what type of cases does the Supreme Court of the United States have original jurisdiction? (Use Constitution of the United States of America or U.S.C.S. or U.S.C.A.)

14. Every bill passed by both Houses must be presented to the President before it becomes law. Two courses of action by the President are prescribed by the Constitution, either of which will result in the bill becoming law. What are they? (Use U.S.C.S.)

15. A Wisconsin compulsory school attendance law requires that Amish children attend high school. Parents of Amish children challenge the statute on the ground that the statute is contrary their religious beliefs. What result? (Use Constitution of the United States of America.)

16. A juvenile is charged with delinquency which may result in commitment. The parents and child are unable to employ counsel. Do they have a right to court-appointed counsel? (Use Constitution of the United States of America.)

17. Who determines when Presidential disability exists under the 25th Amendment? (Use Constitution of the United States of America or U.S.C.S.)

18. May a state grant property tax exemptions to religious organizations for religious properties used solely for worship? (Use Constitution of the United States of America to find case cite.)

19. May Federal judges be removed from office by impeachment? Cite only the correct constitutional provision. (Use Constitution of the United States of America.)

20. The Constitution authorizes the removal of a President by impeachment, brought by the House of Representatives and tried by the Senate. What federal official presides over the trial? (Use Constitution of the United States of America or U.S.C.S. or U.S.C.A.)

ASSIGNMENT 2
UNITED STATES CONSTITUTION

Method:

Using the tables and information contained in The Constitution of the United States of America (Library of Congress, 1987) answer the following questions.

Questions:

1. How many amendments to the Constitution have not been ratified after being submitted to the states?

2. What is the subject of the most recent proposed amendment to the constitution which was submitted to the states for ratification and failed to pass?

3. What is the subject matter of the proposed 27th Amendment to the Constitution?

4. In 1918 the Supreme Court held unconstitutional a statute prohibiting interstate shipment of articles made by child labor. What was the law and the case?

5. What case held unconstitutional the provisions of the Immigration and Naturalization Act of 1952, which provided for revocation of citizenship of those who had voted in a foreign election?

6. The Internal Revenue Code of 1954 had a provision which required gamblers to declare their gambling income. These provisions were held not to prevent the assertion of one's privilege against self-incrimination. Which cases held this?

7. What case held unconstitutional the section of the Voting Rights Act Amendments of 1970 that set the minimum age of 18 in state and local elections?

8. Shapiro v. Thompson, 394 U.S. 618 (1969), held what Act of Congress to be unconstitutional?

9. In what case did the Supreme Court hold that a Virginia statute which prohibited interracial marriages was unconstitutional?

10. What 1824 case held that an Ohio statute levying a tax on the Bank of the United States was unconstitutional?

11. What 1956 case held that an indigent defendant is entitled to a free copy of the entire transcript of his criminal trial under some circumstances?

12. What justices concurred separately in the 1961 Cramp v. Board of

<u>Public Instructions</u> decision which held unconstitutional a law requiring state and local employees to swear that they never lent support to the Communist Party?

13. <u>Gideon v. Wainwright</u>, 372 U.S. 335 (1963), overruled what prior case?

14. <u>Wolf v. Colorado</u>, 338 U.S. 25 (1949), was overruled in part by what 1961 case?

15. <u>West Coast Hotel Co. v. Parrish</u>, 300 U.S. 379 (1937), overruled what case?

ASSIGNMENT 3
COMPARISON OF STATE CONSTITUTIONS

Sources: The constitution of the states to which reference is made in each question.

Index-Digest of State Constitutions (Legislative Drafting Fund of Columbia University, 2d ed., 1959 with 1971 cumulative supplement).

Method:

Briefly answer the questions and cite the applicable constitutional provision.

Questions:

1. May divorces be granted by private, local or special law in:
   Alabama
   Indiana
   Nevada

2. May a person under guardianship vote in:
   Arizona
   Idaho
   Minnesota

3. May legitimation be authorized by local, private or special law in:
   California
   Texas
   Wyoming

4. Is the property of public libraries exempt from taxation in:
   California
   Oklahoma

5. Is a state lottery legal in New York?

6. Do the Nevada and Utah state constitutions define periods of emergency resulting from disasters caused by enemy attack?

7. What constitutional clauses provide a method of invoking initiative and referendum in:
   California
   Michigan
   Nevada

8. Are canals treated as public highways in Arkansas?

9. Does the Louisiana state constitution provide for the payment of a pension to a surviving spouse and minor children of law enforcement officers killed while engaged in the direct apprehension of persons during course of performance of duties?

10. Are military records and relics preserved in the office of the adjutant-general in Idaho?

11. May absconding debtors be imprisoned in Washington and Utah?

12. Are sheriffs commissioned by the governors in Arkansas and Delaware?

13. Is polygamy expressly prohibited by constitutional provision in Utah and Oklahoma?

14. Are perpetuities allowable for eleemosynary purposes in Montana?

15. Are retrospective laws permissible in:
    Colorado
    Tennessee
    Texas

16. How are claims brought against the state in:
    Arizona
    Washington
    Wisconsin

17. What constitutes a woman's separate property in:
    Alabama
    Michigan
    Utah

18. In case of suicide how does property descend in:
    Colorado
    Delaware
    Texas

19. What does the Michigan constitution provide with respect to findings of fact in workmen's compensation proceedings?

20. What does the Wyoming constitution provide with respect to the make up of Congressional districts?

ASSIGNMENT 4
STATE CONSTITUTIONS -- INDEXES

Sources: The general index to the appropriate state statutes, index to the constitution, topical analysis of separate articles, and notes to the decisions of each state to which reference is made.

Method:

Using the above sources, cite the applicable constitutional provision for each question below.

1. Cite the Maine constitutional provision dealing with construction of buildings for industrial use.

2. The Maine legislature's authority to insure Maine veterans' mortgage loans up to eighty percent.

3. The Main constitution includes a provision which amends the apportionment of senatorial districts beginning in 1983.

4. Cite the Wyoming constitutional article dealing with changing the names of persons or places.

5. Can a woman under the age of fourteen do clerical work at a mine in Wyoming?

6. Is there a limitation on municipal indebtedness for the purpose of building sewers in Wyoming?

7. Does the U.S. government have jurisdiction over Indian land in Wyoming?

8. Does the schedule of the Tennessee constitution of 1870 provide for the appointment of a state reporter?

9. In Tennessee, can the size of an existing county be reduced to less that 275 square miles?

10. Which section of the Tennessee constitution deals with the pay and allowances for members of the General Assembly?

ASSIGNMENT 5
STATE CONSTITUTIONS -- CONSTRUCTION

Method:

Using bound volumes, bound supplements, specific pamphlet supplements, pocket parts, and general pamphlet supplements to the appropriate state statutes, cite the cases and answer the questions given below.

Questions:

1. With reference to your answer of Question 1, Assignment 4 above, cite the Maine authority fixing the minimum limit on percentage of voters who may authorize issuance of municipal bonds, below which the Legislature may not go.

2. Cite a 1975 Maine authority construing Article IV, part 1, section 8 of the Maine Constitution.

3. With reference to your answer to the same section of the Wyoming Constitution given in your answer to Question 4, Assignment 4, cite a Wyoming case holding that because a statute applies only to one city it is not necessarily unconstitutional as special legislation.

4. Article 9 of the Wyoming Constitution has a section which discusses the position of inspector of mines. In the "cross references" annotation to the section, two cases are listed. When were these two cases decided? Cite the older case.

5. With reference to the same section of the Wyoming Constitution given in your answer to Question 6, Assignment 4 above, cite a 1966 Wyoming case discussing storm sewers and additional bonded indebtedness.

6. With reference to your answer to Question 7, Assignment 4 above, cite the case which discusses power dam construction on former Indian lands.

7. With reference to the Sixth Amendment of the United States Constitution, cite the Tennessee case holding that a defendant's right to a speedy trial was not prejudiced even if he was not arrested immediately, because the evidence clearly showed that efforts were initiated to locate him within hours after the cirme was committed.

8. With reference to the same section of the Tennessee Constitution given in your answer to Question 9, Assignment 4 above, cite the 1917 Tennessee case indicating whether the size of a county of less than 500 square miles could be further reduced.

9. With reference to your answer to Question 10, Assignment 4 above, cite the 1974 Tennessee case which discusses the state general assembly.

10. When (if ever) was that section of the New Mexico Constitution dealing with the right to bear arms most recently amended?

ASSIGNMENT 6
THEME PROBLEMS AND DRILL PROBLEMS

Theme Problem I:

1. What parts of the U.S. Constitution does Brown v. Board of Education (347 U.S. 483) discuss?

2. Name four places where one could locate those sections.

3. What is the advantage of an annotated constitution?

4. Using U.S.C.A., find discussion of the Brown decision under the Equal Protection point of the 14th Amendment. Under what heading and number does it appear?

5. How can one get into such specialized areas when there are so many cases digested?

6. Using U.S.C.S., find discussion of the Brown decision under the Equal Protection Clause of the 14th Amendment. Under what heading and number does it appear?

7. Using U.S.C.S., where could one find cases on discrimination in colleges and universities?

8. Using U.S.C.S., does the bound volume cite any Annotations on the topic of Brown?

9. Using U.S.C.S., if one wanted to find related law review articles, where could one look?

10. Using the Library of Congress Constitution of the United States of America (1987), locate discussion of the Brown case. On what pages is it discussed?

11. How does the discussion found in Question 10 differ from those found in U.S.C.A. and U.S.C.S.?

12. What problems would be presented by using the Library of Congress edition?

Theme Problem II:

1. What part of the Constitution does Roe v. Wade (410 U.S. 113) rely upon?

2. Name four places where you could find the text involved.

3. What would be the advantage of using an annotated constitution?

4. Using the U.S.C.A. Constitution volumes to answer Questions 4-7,

where can one find discussion of the Roe case under the heading of Abortions - generally.

5. What case is noted before it?

6. How many places would you have to check to be sure you have all current cases on the subject?

7. Where could one find cases on the regulation of the advertising of contraceptives?

8. Using the Constitution volumes of U.S.C.S. for Questions 8-11, where in the notes could you find the Roe decision digested as a criminal matter?

9. Where could one find related law review articles?

10. Cite a relevant Annotation.

11. What does the abbreviation "LC" mean?

12. Contrast the information found through U.S.C.A. and U.S.C.S.; which is more useful and why?

13. Is Roe v. Wade discussed in the Constitution of the United States of America (1972 ed.) by the Library of Congress?

14. Does your home state have a constitutional provision on abortion? If so, cite and state its status.

Drill Problem I:

A. Using the Library of Congress Constitution of the United States of America (1987 ed.), answer the following:

1. The 1941 decision in United States v. Classic, 313 U.S. 299, overruled what former decision?

2. What is the only place in the Constitution where the writ of habeas corpus is mentioned?

3. What case held the Act of Aug. 24, 1935 (49 Stat. 750) unconstitutional as beyond the taxing power?

4. What doctrine did the court establish in the case of Luther v. Borden, 48 U.S. 1 (1849)?

B. Use the Constitution as printed in the U.S.C.A. or the U.S.C.S. to answer the following:

1. What article and section of the Constitution deals with the power of Congress to declare war?

2. What provision empowers Congress to define what constitutes piracy and to set punishments for it?

3. What provision prohibits states from keeping ships of war without the consent of Congress?

4. Which provision guarantees a trial by jury in criminal cases? Locate a 1953 decision from the Sixth Circuit which holds that the elements of a constitutional jury trial that require 12 jurors and a unanimous verdict are procedural and not jurisdictional.

5. What provision gives Congress the power to grant copyrights?

Drill Problem II:

A. Using the Library of Congress Constitution of the United States of America (1987 ed.), answer the following:

1. The 1890 decision of Leisy v. Hardin, 135 U.S. 100 (1890) overruled an Iowa law dealing with what subject matter?

2. Where can discussion of Ng Fung Ho v. White, 259 U.S. 276 (1922) be found?

3. Has there been a great deal of judicial commentary concerning the Third Amendment?

4. Which Supreme Court case dealt with the conviction of a man wearing a flag sewn to the seat of his trousers?

B. Use the Constitution as printed in U.S.C.A. or U.S.C.S. to answer the following:

1. Which Amendment prevents a criminal defendant from having to face the same charges twice?

2. Cite a 1978 federal decision from an Alabama case holding that intent is a necessary element in an action for racial gerrymandering under the XV Amendment.

3. Where is it specified that two witnesses are needed to convict a person of treason?

4. What provision prevents a religious test from ever being applied as a requirement for any office in the federal government?

Drill Problem III:

A. Using the Library of Congress Constitution of the United States of America (1987 ed.), answer the following:

1. What was the first territory (later a state) to accord full suffrage rights to women in 1869, presaging the Nineteenth Amendment?

2. How many amendments to the Constitution have been submitted to the states and have failed to be ratified?

3. What is the object of the clause requiring Congress to keep a journal?

4. Was a statute that denied polygamists the right to vote in territorial elections unconstitutional as an ex post facto law when applied to one who had not contracted a polygamous marriage since the passing of the act?

5. Where can one locate discussion of the doctrine of prior restraint as it applies to the First Amendment?

B. Use the Constitution as printed in U.S.C.A. or U.S.C.S. to answer the following:

1. What part of the Constitution mandates the taking of a national census at 10 year intervals?

2. What provisions deal with taxation of native Americans?

3. Where is the pardon power of the President created?

4. Which clause of the Constitution deals with habeas corpus?

CHAPTER 9

FEDERAL LEGISLATION

ASSIGNMENT 1
FEDERAL LEGISLATION - PARALLEL REFERENCE TABLES: U.S.C.

Method:

Using the parallel reference tables of the United States Code, the United States Code annotated, or the United States Code Service, give the U.S.C. citation for each of the public public laws.

Questions:

1. 92-230
2. 93-387
3. 91-586
4. 90-81
5. 90-619 sec. 1
6. 89-589
7. 89-29
8. 86-591
9. 94-209
10. 94-241
11. 87-824
12. 97-62
13. 98-167
14. 95-175

ASSIGNMENT 2
FEDERAL LEGISLATION - PARALLEL REFERENCE TABLES: U.S.C.C.A.N.

Method:

Using the Table of Classifications in the U.S. Code Congressional and Administrative News, give the U.S.C. citation for each of the following public laws:

Questions:

1. 89-360
2. 89-586
3. 89-615
4. 89-771
5. 90-66
6. 90-118
7. 90-194
8. 90-330
9. 90-498
10. 90-597
11. 91-5
12. 91-154
13. 91-233
14. 91-300
15. 95-233
16. 95-415
17. 97-62
18. 97-275
19. 98-81
20. 98-217
21. 99-59
22. 99-258
23. 100-174
24. 100-633
25. 100-695

ASSIGNMENT 3
UNITED STATES CODE CONGRESSIONAL AND ADMINISTRATIVE NEWS: USE OF THE INDEX TO LOCATE ACTS

Method:

Using the index to the U.S. Code Congressional and Administrative News, give the number of the Senate or House bill, the Public Law number and the approval date of the Act.

Questions:

A. 1969 volumes:

1. Providing for a national center on educational media and materials for the handicapped.
2. Protection of children from hazardous toys.
3. Establishing a national policy for the environment.
4. Establishment of a Commission on Government Procurement.
5. Increasing the rates of dependency and indemnity compensation payable to widows of veterans.

B. 1970 volumes:

1. Special packaging to protect children from ingestion of poisons.
2. Disposition of geothermal steam resources.
3. Prohibiting the movement in interstate commerce of "sored" horses.
4. Rate of duty on parts of stethoscopes.
5. Continuation of the International Coffee Agreement Act of 1968.

C. 1980 volumes:

1. Establishing national poison prevention week.
2. Providing for construction, reconstruction and renovation of academic buildings.
3. Regulation of saccharin.
4. Prevention of kidnapping by parents.
5. Dealing with insect, fungus, and rodent control.

D. 1986 volumes:

1. Reporting hours of employment of batboys and batgirls.
2. Relating to actions against the United States to quiet title.
3. Establishing privacy of electronic communications.
4. Designing system of fair debt collection practices for attorneys.
5. Establishing national marketing quotas for tobacco and tobacco products.

E. 1988 volumes:

1. Protecting and managing archeological resources.
2. Price supports for the cotton industry.
3. Regulating use of degradable plastic ring carriers.
4. Health and accident insurance for temporary federal employees.
5. Establishing a fishing agreement with the Soviet Union.

ASSIGNMENT 4
LOCATING A RECENT STATUTE IN THE U.S. CODE BY USE OF THE INDEX

Sources: United States Code, 1988 Edition

United States Code Annotated

United States Code Service

Method:

(1) Briefly answer the question.

(2) Use any of the above sources and cite the relevant title and section of the United States Code and the latest Statutes at Large.

Questions:

1. What is the maximum penalty for violation of the labeling requirement of the Public Health Cigarette Smoking Act of 1969?

2. Who fixes the per anum rates of basic pay of positions on the National Zoological Park police force?

3. Is the Secretary of Agriculture authorized to eradicate the golden nematode?

4. May Coast Guard warrant officers be temporarily promoted to higher warrant officer grades?

5. Are the natives of the Pribilof Islands entitled by law to receive free dental care from the United States government.

6. What is the maximum penalty for impersonating, falsely and with intent to defraud, an agent for the 4-H clubs.

7. May the Secretary of the Smithsonian Institution authorize the employment of aliens?

8. What is the minimum age at which Indians have the right to receive annuity money due them?

9. Do provisions of the Occupational Safety and Health Act of 1970 apply to employment performed in the Canal Zone?

10. Do provisions of the Age Discrimination in Employment Act of 1967 apply to persons between the ages of 35-39?

11. Geothermal leases are for a primary term of how many years?

12. Can instructors of the National Guard use public buildings for their offices?

13. How many members are authorized for the National Advisory Committee on Oceans and Atmosphere?

14. May the Paralyzed Veterans of America promote the candidacy of a person for public office?

15. The United States Postal Service was established as an independent establishment of which branch of the U.S. government?

16. May an employee of the Capitol Guide Service accept a gratuity for his official services?

17. Can the Secretary of State accept money and property as gifts to carry out the purposes of the Center for Cultural and Technical Interchange between East and West?

18. Is California considered a Colorado River Basin State under provisions of the Colorado River Basin Project Act.?

19. How many members of the general public are selected to sit on the Technical Pipeline Safety Standards Committee, which deals with natural gas?

20. Under provisions of the Federal Contested Elections Act, must service of the notice of contest upon contestee be made only by delivering a copy to him personally?

ASSIGNMENT 5
TABLES OF POPULAR NAMES OF FEDERAL ACTS

Sources: United States Code, 1982 edition, Index of Acts Cited by Popular Name.

United States Code Service, Lawyers' Edition. Tables. (1985)

United States Code Annotated, General Index.

Shepard's Acts and Cases by Popular Names. (1986)

Method:

(1) Using source No. 1 above, give the citation to the first Statutes at Large enactment and to the U.S. Code, by title and first section, as well as the page number of the table where the Act is located.

(2) Using sources 2 and 3 above, indicate only the page on which the Act is located in each source.

(3) Using source 4 above, list the first reference which is provided.

Questions:

1. Age Discrimination in Employment Act of 1967.
2. Bilingual Education Act.
3. Commodity Credit Corporation Charter Act.
4. Environmental Education Act.
5. Export Apple and Pear Act.
6. Federal Contested Election Act.
7. Gambling Devices Act of 1962.
8. Handicapped Children's Early Education Assistance Act.
9. International Organizations Immunities Act.
10. Jury Selection and Service Act of 1968.
11. Motor Vehicle Air Pollution Control Act.
12. National Commission on Libraries and Information Science Act.
13. National Portrait Gallery Act.
14. National Trails System Act.

15. Newspaper Preservation Act.

16. Public Broadcasting Financing Act of 1970.

17. Radiation Control for Health and Safety Act of 1968.

18. Service Contract Act of 1965.

19. Special Drawing Rights Act.

20. Standard Reference Data Act.

ASSIGNMENT 6
FEDERAL LEGISLATION - CODE ANNOTATIONS

Method:

Each of the problems below contains a reference to a particular title and section of the United States Code. Each such section has been interpreted by the courts. Annotations on a case interpreting a particular section will follow that section in the United States Code Annotated. Using these annotations, answer the questions in the problems below. Cite a case supporting your answer.

Questions:

1. Categories of priorities for visas for potential immigrants to this country are set out in 8 U.S.C. Sec. 1153. Subsection (a)(3) gives the third priority to immigrants who are members of the professions. Who bears the burden of proof with respect to a third preference visa?

2. The hunting of migratory birds, except as provided by regulation, is outlawed by 16 U.S.C. Sec. 703. Is the red-tailed hawk a migratory bird?

3. A remedy is provided by 25 U.S.C. Sec. 229 for U.S. citizens who have suffered injuries to their property at the hands of an Indian belonging to a tribe in "amity" with the United States. What constitutes "amity" as it is used in this section?

4. Certain disruptive students are disqualified by 20 U.S.C. Sec. 1088f from participation in federal student assistance programs. Has the constitutionality of this section ever been tested?

5. All citizens of the U.S. are given the same right to buy and sell property as the white citizen has by 42 U.S.C. Sec. 1982. Has this section ever been held to apply to a cemetery lot?

6. Voting qualifications which are designed to deny citizens the right to vote on account of race are prohibited by 42 U.S.C. Sec. 1973. Has this section ever been given retroactive effect?

7. Slavery in the United States was abolished by 42 U.S.C. Sec. 1994. Would that provision outlaw assignment of attorneys to represent indigents without compensation?

8. Discrimination and segregation in public places are prohibited by 42 U.S.C. Sec. 2000a. Would this prohibition apply to a skating rink?

9. In order to collect social security disability benefits, one's disability must fall within the definition of "disability" given in 42 U.S.C. Sec. 423(d). Could a psychosomatic impairment satisfy this definition?

10. Those persons who may be punished as principals for violations of federal criminal statutes are set out in 18 U.S.C. Sec.2. Could an officer who agreed to protect a criminal be punished as a principal?

11. Is laches likely to be a good defense to a charge of conspiracy under 18 U.S.C. Sec. 371?

12. In determining the eligibility for parole under 18 U.S.C. Sec. 4202, is it proper to aggregate sentences which are being served consecutively?

13. Would 18 U.S.C. Sec. 1341, outlawing the use of the mails to execute a scheme to defraud, include premarital promises?

14. The procedure for removal of cases from state courts to federal district courts is provided by 28 U.S.C. Sec. 1446. May the bond required by this section be waived?

15. It is provided by 28 U.S.C. Sec. 2246 that on an application for a writ of habeas corpus, evidence may be taken by deposition. What law governs the taking of such a deposition?

ASSIGNMENT 7
USE OF U.S.C.S., UNCODIFIED LAWS AND TREATIES VOLUME

Sources: United States Code Service, Lawyers' Edition. Notes to Uncodified Laws and Treaties.

Method:

Cite a case interpreting the uncodified Federal law.

Questions:

1. The words "hereby granted" in the settlement and preemption proviso of the Joint Resolution, approved May 31, 1870, 16 Stat. 378, applied only to lands within the place limits in the State of Montana and not to lands acquired by the Northern Pacific Railway within the "second indemnity strip" in that state.

2. Note given to the United States and representing feed and seed loan made pursuant to the Joint Resolution, approved December 20, 1930, c. 21, 46 Stat. 1032, was not barred by state statute of limitations or by laches.

3. The three-mile limit of territorial waters jurisdiction of the United States in preventing the smuggling of intoxicating liquors are limited by a treaty with Great Britain to a three-mile limit in territorial waters and seizure 20 miles from shore is unlawful (43 Stat. 1761).

4. United States succeeded to sovereignty of California by the Treaty of Guadalupe Hidalgo and had authority to impose a registration act on claimants to California land, under Act of March 3, 1851, c. 41, 9 Stat. 631.

5. The Menominee Indians, being dissatisfied with an arrangement made in 1822 to cede a large tract of land for the use of other tribes, agreed by a treaty at 7 Stat. 303 (1827) to refer the issue to the President.

6. The Wyoming Admission Act of July 10, 1890, c. 664, 26 Stat. 222 did not give the title to the lands identified as sections 16 and 36 upon the approval and acceptance of the official resurveys made by the general land office designating the lands in question as sections 16 and 36.

7. One charged with a sale of less than a gallon of intoxicating liquor can be compelled to submit to finger printing under the Jones Act amendments, 46 Stat. 1036 (1931).

8. An agreement between the city of San Francisco and the Secretary of the Interior, relieving the obligation to reimburse the U.S. for maintenance of certain roads in Yosemite National Park, under the Act of Dec. 19, 1913, c. 4, 38 Stat. 242, was void and the U.S. was not estopped from disaffirming the agreement.

9. Where Select Committee on Presidential Campaign Activities sought

declaration from District Court pursuant to Pub. L. No. 93-190, 87 Stat. 736 (1973), that President Nixon had a legal duty to comply with a subpoena duces tecum directing him to produce five taped conversations and had its dismissed complaint affirmed.

10. The House Committee on Un-American Activities was not authorized under the Legislative Reorganization Act of August 2, 1946, C. 753, 60 Stat. 816, Section 121 to conduct an investigation in Puerto Rico.

11. Act of June 14, 1926, ch. 582, 44 Stat. 744 (1926) gave all title and interest in the bridge across Port Washington Narrows to the state by purchase or condemnation proceedings.

12. The property of the City of Dubuque Bridge Commission established by the Act of July 18, 1939, c. 318, 53 Stat. 1051 is not immune from state real estate tax.

13. Tax paid under protest under the Act of Feb. 10, 1936, c. 42, 49 Stat. 1106, could be recovered upon the tax and the act being held unconstitutional.

14. Section 9(a) of the Teton Dam Disaster Assistance Act, 90 Stat. 1211 (1976), was intended to establish independence of claims under the Act from those that might exist under any other provision of applicable law and does not waive the filing requirements of the Federal Tort Claims Act.

15. The State of New Mexico may pledge lands to carry out provisions of the Act of May 28, 1928, c. 812, 45 Stat. 775.

16. A bridge across Sandusky Bay was held taxable as real property under the Act of May 5, 1926, c. 245, 44 Stat. 402.

17. The provision as to search of private dwellings under the Willis-Campbell Act of Nov. 23, 1921, c. 134, 42 Stat. 223, Section 3 applied to Alaska.

18. The Soldiers' and Sailors' Civil Relief Act of March 8, 1918, c. 20, 40 Stat. 440, Section 102, was held to apply to proceedings in state courts.

19. The Food Control, "Lever Act" of Aug. 10, 1917, c. 53, 40 Stat. 276, was held not to have suspended operation of state antitrust laws.

20. The Indian Depredation Claims Act of Jan. 11, 1915, c. 7, 38 Stat. 791, did not reinstate claims previously dismissed on grounds other than alienage of claimant.

ASSIGNMENT 8
USE OF TABLES FROM FORMER TITLES OF U.S. CODE TO PRESENT TITLE

Source: United States Code Annotated. 1984 Cumulative Supplement Tables volume.

Method:

Refer to U.S.C.A. Revised Titles Tables. The problems relate to former sections. Give either the current section number of the revised title or the present status of the former section.

Questions:

1. 53, T.11
2. 526, T.34
3. 630h, T.5
4. 1014, T.31
5. 964, T.39
6. 101, T.11
7. 2, T.46
8. 104, T.10
9. 310, T.37
10. 32, T.17
11. 286, T.44
12. 67, T.49
13. 533, T.11
14. 556, T.11
15. 573, T.11

ASSIGNMENT 9
THEME PROBLEMS AND DRILL PROBLEMS

Theme Problem I:

A. 18 U.S.C. 245 proscribes willful interference with anyone's right to a public education on the basis of race. Using the U.S.C., locate that provision and answer the following:

1. What was the Public Law number of this legislation?

2. Give its Statutes at Large citation.

3. What is the fine imposed if bodily injury results?

4. If you own and occupy a home with four rooms for hire, are you bound by the law in renting the other units?

B. Using U.S.C.A., find the same provision and answer the following:

1. Have any cases been decided under Sec. 245?

2. Cite a case that involved threats to a presidential candidate.

3. Has Title 18 been enacted into positive law?

C. Using U.S.C.S., find the same provision and answer the following:

1. Into what three sets does it give you research entry?

2. Does 18 U.S.C. Sec. 245 create a civil cause of action? Cite a case.

3. Does U.S.C.A. or U.S.C.S. seem more useful? Why?

D. The 93rd Congress, 2nd Session, passed legislation that all children, regardless of race, color, sex, or national origin, are entitled to equal educational opportunities in the public schools. Find this legislation and answer the following using the appropriate U.S. Statutes at Large volume.

1. What is the short title of this Act?

2. What is the name and citation of the larger Act of which it is a part?

3. What was the bill number of the Act?

4. Where is Title II codified in U.S.C.?

Theme Problem II:

A. The plaintiffs and intervenor in Roe v. Wade appealed to the U.S. Supreme Court under 28 U.S.C. Sec. 1253. Examine that provision in the U.S.C. and answer the following:

Chapter 9

1. What was the U.S. Statutes at Large citation for this legislation?

2. Where would one look for related sections on writs?

3. Where else in the title is this section referred to?

4. What are the appendices to Title 28?

B. Using U.S.C.A., look up the same provision and answer the following:

1. What Key Numbers apply?

2. Where are cases on the question of "mootness" noted?

3. Where are cases on the courts of Puerto Rico noted?

C. Using U.S.C.S., look up the same provision and answer these questions:

1. Cite a law review article by Rosenberg on this topic.

2. To what two sets of forms are you given citations?

3. Where are cases on the order of a single judge court noted?

D. Compare and contrast the advantages of the three tools used above.\

E. The 94th Congress, 1st Session, passed legislation which forbade any officer or employee of the United States to coerce anyone to have an abortion. Find that legislation using the appropriate U.S. Statutes at Large volume and answer the following:

1. What is the name and citation of the act?

2. What was its Senate bill number?

3. Where will the section on coercion appear in U.S.C.?

Theme Problem III:

A. What is the provision of the U.S.C. which deals with the adequate representation of criminal defendants through authorizing each U.S. District Court to draw up a plan?

B. Turn to that provision in U.S.C. and answer the following:

1. What is the maximum total amount an appointed attorney may receive in a felony case?

2. What was the U.S. Statutes at Large Act upon which this section is based?

3. What was the effective date of the 1974 amendment?

C. Using U.S.C.A., locate this provision and answer the following:

1. What Key Number will lead to relevant cases?

2. Does the pocket part contain new text? If so, what legislation is the changed text based upon?

D. Using U.S.C.S., locate the same provision and answer the following:

1. Cite a relevant law review article by Professor Tague.

2. Find a case that decides if the "expert services" made available under subsection 18(e) comprehend psychiatric assistance.

E. Compare and contrast U.S.C., U.S.C.A., and U.S.C.S. as to how easy you find them to use.

F. The 91st Congress, 2nd Session, passed legislation that changed the name of the D.C. Legal Aid Agency and redefined its structure and function. Find that legislation using the appropriate U.S. Statutes at Large volume and answer the following:

1. What is the title and citation of the act of which it is a part?

2. Which title of the act deals with the Public Defender Service?

3. Where will these provisions be codified?

Drill Problem I:

A. Using either the U.S.C., U.S.C.A., or U.S.C.S., answer the following:

1. Where in the Code would one find the penalty for the forgery of a passport?

2. Where in the Code is the law affecting the issuance of commercial licenses by the Nuclear Regulatory Commission?

3. What section of the Code gives the sentence for a U.S. ship captain who voluntarily surrenders his ship to a pirate?

4. What section of the Code requires state legislatures and officers to declare allegiance to the Constitution of the United States?

5. Where in the Code does it calculate the average rate of interest of the reserves of a life insurance company?

B. Using any of the popular name tables, locate the correct citation for the following (it may be necessary to consult more than one):

1. White Russian Act

2. Dawson Act

3. Wetback Act

4. Maritime Extension Act

5. American Fire Act

C. For each of the questions in this section, provide:

(1) The Public Law (or Chapter) number and Statutes at Large citation for the original legislation described.

(2) The location of the legislation in the U.S. Code. (Note: if it has not been codified, write "none." If it has been codified in several Code locations, list the citation for the earliest part of the Act codified.)

1. What 1975 act provides indemnity for creative works that are displayed in exhibitions?

2. What act passed by the 90th Congress prescribes penalties for the violation of certain federally protected rights of an individual?

3. What act passed by the 93rd Congress enables females to participate in National Little League baseball?

4. What act passed by the 85th Congress authorizes construction of the U.S.S. Arizona Memorial?

5. What act passed by the 93rd Congress provides financial assistance to prevent child abuse?

Drill Problem II:

A. Using U.S.C., U.S.C.A., or U.S.C.S., answer the following:

1. What are the factors determining whether a particular piece of work could be reproduced under the "fair use" doctrine?

2. What section of the code declares United States cooperation with other countries in the control of narcotics?

3. What section of the code specifies the age limits of those liable for training and service in a military draft?

4. What is the punishment for the disclosure of information involving U.S. communication of intelligence to aid a foreign country?

5. What sections of the code authorize the Secretary of Labor to recruit agricultural workers from Mexico?

B. Using any of the popular name tables, locate the correct citation for the following:

1. Bloody Bill Act

2. Shingles Quota Act

3. Sac and Fox Allotment Act

4. Refugee Asistance Act

5. Failing Newspaper Act

C. For each of the questions in this section, provide:

(1) The Public Law (or Chapter) number and Statutes at Large citation for the original legislation described.

(2) The location of the legislation in the U.S.C. (Note: if it has not been codified, write "none." If it has been codified in several locations in the Code, list the citation for the earliest part of the Act codified.)

1. What act passed by the 93rd Congress provides job training for the economically disadvantaged and underemployed?

2. What act was passed in 1954 to modify and extend the existing national defense laws?

3. What act restored citizenship, posthumously, to Robert E. Lee in 1975.

4. What act provides for the establishment of an American Folklife Center in the Library of Congress?

5. What act of the 93rd Congress provides for the protection of human subjects in biomedical research?

Drill Problem III:

A. Using U.S.C., U.S.C.A., or U.S.C.S., answer the following:

1. What are the testing requirements to determine whether a substance causes cancer?

2. Where in the code is a study of the protection of whales?

3. Where in the code is the definition of "misleading advertisement"?

4. Where in the code is an employee's right to organize a labor union affirmed?

B. Using any of the popular name tables, locate the correct citation for the following (it may be necessary to consult more than one):

1. Chace Act

2. Stowaways Act

3. Coercive Practices Act

4. Sunshine Law

5. Filled Cheese Act

C. For each of the questions in this section, provide:

(1) The Public Law (or Chapter) number and Statutes at Large citation for the original legislation described.

(2) The location of the legislation in U.S.C. (Note: if it has not been codified, write "none." If it has been codified in several parts of the code, list the citation for the earliest part of the Act codified.)

1. What 1973 Act amends the Public Service Act in order to encourage the operation of health maintenance organizations?

2. What 1972 Act authorizes the Atomic Energy Commission to issue temporary operating licenses for nuclear power plants?

3. What 1942 joint resolution declared a state of war against the government of Hungary?

4. What 1975 Act established the Hells Canyon National Recreation Area?

5. What Act of the 85th Congress allowed the duty-free importation of religious regalia when it was presented free of charge to a church?

CHAPTER 10

FEDERAL LEGISLATIVE HISTORIES

Introduction:

The questions presented here were developed to involve the use of the five sources for legislative histories most commonly found in small to medium-sized libraries. Students should become aware of other sources such as the U.S. Library of Congress, Congressional Research Service, Digest of Public General Bills; U.S. Congress, House of Representatives, Numerical Order of Bills and Resolutions which have passed either or both Houses, and Bills now pending on the Calendar; U.S. Congress, Senate, Library, Cumulative Index of Congressional Hearings, Bill Number Index; Public Laws (slip laws). The questions were set up to include long and short questions in each section so that students may be assigned a long and a short question in each section as well as one or more of the general questions appearing at the end.

ASSIGNMENT 1
CONGRESSIONAL INFORMATION SERVICE

Method:

Use Congressional Information Service Annuals, 1970-75, Index volumes and tables of bill numbers, Abstract volumes and legislative histories. Answers to all questions should be cited according to rules in the latest edition of A Uniform System Of Citation, limiting citations to information found in C.I.S. Include volume, year, and pages where answers are found.

Questions:

1. In 1976 legislation was enacted to extend the United States fishing limit to 200 miles to prevent foreign over-fishing off the United States coast. President Ford supported the legislation on the condition that its effective date would be delayed so that the Law of the Sea Conference could complete its work. To trace the history of the current legislation, find the following in the 1975 CIS volumes:
   (a) Senate Report of H.R. 200, 94th Congress, 1st Session. Cite report and name of committee reporting.
   (b) What CIS Abstract number would you use to find the special oversight report on H.R. 200 on microfiche?
   (c) What are the numbers of the three House bills requiring the employment of straight baselines in charting fishery zone boundaries?

2. The Environmental Protection Agency was authorized to conduct research on the effects of noise on animals, humans and property, and one of the provisions H.R. 11,021, as cleared by Congress on October 18, 1972, made it

unlawful to import excessively noisy products. You wish to read some of the testimony presented before the Senate Committee by John Tyler, head of the technical committee of the National Organization to Insure the Sound Controlled Environment, and the floor debates on the bills. Cite:

(a) Public Law number.
(b) Date of enactment, Statutes at Large and Congressional Record citation, Senate Hearings wherein Mr. Tyler's testimony is recorded, the Presidential Statement of October 28, 1972.
(c) Name of the House committee which reported on H.R. 11,021 and the House report number.

3. Organized crime control legislation (Bomb Threat Act) was proposed in S. 30 in 1969 and 1970. You wish to read the congressional hearing of June 11, 1970, during which examples of activities of organized crime which could be prevented under the bill's provisions, such as the racketeering operations of the Mafia, the Marcello organization in New Orleans, and newspaper articles on infiltration of legitimate business by organized crime were introduced. Find:
   (a) Public Law number of the Act.
   (b) Date of enactment, Statutes at Large and Congressional Record citations. State the name of the Senate committee reporting, and the CIS Abstract number of the House hearing.
   (c) Cite House Report and Congress which recommended passage of the bill, and the name of the member of the House of Representatives from New York who stated that the bill was unconstitutional.

4. In 1968 Congress repealed the authority which had been given o the National Science Foundation in 1958 to require persons engaging in weather modification activities to report such activities. This was repealed, and in 1971 legislation was enacted to require reporting of weather modification activities to the Federal government. To research the need for H.R. 6893, and the possibility of future legal and international problems arising from weather modification, find the following:
   (a) Public Law number.
   (b) Statutes at Large and Congressional Record citations. CIS Abstract numbers for the House hearings.
   (c) Cite the hearings.

5. In 1973 legislation was enacted to amend the Lead Based Paint Poisoning Act to prohibit the use of lead based paint in construction of facilities and in the manufacture of certain toys and utensils. Cite the following legislative materials in connection with S. 607:
   (a) Public Law number.
   (b) Date of enactment, Statutes at Large and Congressional Record citation, Number of 1973 Senate Report, and CIS Abstract number for microfiche.
   (c) Cite the House Conference Report which included agreements to differences concerning definitions of lead content constituting a hazard, and Congress.

6. One of the purposes of the Deepwater Port Act of 1974 is to authorize and regulate the location, ownership, construction, and operation of deepwater ports in waters beyond the territorial limits of the United States. Any

adjacent coastal state directly connected by pipeline to a deepwater port is affected by the Act. You are required to research further reasons for the legislation introduced in H.R. 10,701 and H.R. 11,951. Cite:
(a) Public Law number.
(b) Date of enactment, Statutes at Large citation. CIS Abstract number of the 1974 House committee print and the Presidential statement.
(c) Cite Senate committee before which hearings were held.
(d) Title of Senate committee print on policy issues.

7. In December, 1971, legislation was enacted to amend the Fishermen's Protective Act of 1967 to enhance the effectiveness of international fishery conservation programs. The legislation, which had been proposed in H.R. 3304 and related bills, authorized the President to prohibit importation of fishery products from nations conducting fishery operations in a manner that diminishes effectiveness of international fishery conservation programs. Cite legislative materials in support of the above:
(a) Public Law number.
(b) Date of enactment, Statutes at Large and Congressional Record citations. To read the House hearings on microfiche, which CIS Abstract number would you need? Cite the House report.
(c) The hearings also included oversight of Soviet fishing violations in the Atlantic. Where were the hearings of April 14, 1971 held, and before which House committee and subcommittee?

8. Find a discussion of the 1973 planned cut in United States aid to the United Nations, and the extent of and need for assistance to smaller international organizations. Cite Congressional hearing and CIS Abstract number for microfiche.

9. To support their argument that plaintiff satisfied the first requirement for determining a cause of action to be implied in 18 U.S.C. Sec. 610, the U. S. Circuit Court of Appeals, in a 1975 case, referred to the intent of the 1971 legislation which led to the Federal Election Campaign Act. To read Richard G. Kleindienst's testimony regarding political campaign spending before a Senate committee in March 1971, cite the hearing and the CIS Abstract number of the microfiche.

10. In 1972, H.R. 9936 was enacted to provide for a current listing of each drug manufactured. What is the Public Law number? What is the name of the President of the Pharmaceutical Manufacturers' Association who testified in support of the bill? Cite the hearing.

ASSIGNMENT 2
UNITED STATES MONTHLY CATALOG

Method:

Use the subject, title, author index entry numbers of the United States Monthly Catalog, 1970-76, to find Congressional hearings, reports, documents, committee prints, and publications issued by the United States Government Printing Office for the various agencies and departments. Give complete citations in accordance with the latest edition of A Uniform System of Citation.

Question:

1. In December 1975, Public Law No. 94-135, Older Americans Amendments of 1975, was enacted to improve legal representation for older Americans. You wish to procure copies of the congressional material dealing with legislation on the aged and the aging from your congressman. Use the 1976 subject index and cite:
   (a) The Senate committees before which joint hearings were held. Include Congress, session, and date.
   (b) Locate a committee print in the title index which deals with doctors and nurses in nursing home care. Give complete citation.

2. In 1971 Congressional hearings were released on the establishment of a seaward boundary of the continental shelf, and on the emplacement of nuclear weapons on the ocean floor. Cite:
   (a) The hearings on the seaward boundary.
   (b) The Senate Executive Document containing the text of a message from the President on the seabed arms control treaty.

3. The only major Congressional action in 1973 on the busing of school children to eliminate racial segregation was in the form of proposed constitutional amendments prohibiting busing. Give complete citations for both publications:
   (a) A list of publications on constitutional rights was prepared by a subcommittee of the Senate Committee on the Judiciary.
   (b) A list of leading court decisions on public school desegregation was printed for the House Committee on the Judiciary.

4. In 1974 the House failed to act on H.R. 12,462, which established procedures for judicial enforcement of Congress's right to obtain information from federal officials by amending the Freedom of Information Act (Pub. L. No. 89-487). The bill raised the question of whether Congress should set up a statutory mechanism for dealing with claims of executive privilege and thereby implicitly recognize the privilege in law. Cite the following materials on the proposed amendments:
   (a) The report from the committee to accompany H.R. 12,462.
   (b) Hearing on government information involving national security.

5. In fiscal year 1975 business failures were 45% higher than in the previous year. New York's financial crisis and the great increase in the number of business and individual bankruptcies caused Congress to review the

bankruptcy system. Legislation which was introduced in two important bills met with strong resistance from creditors. Many hearings were held in both Houses of Congress. To read the legislative materials on the Bankruptcy Reform Act which were available at the end of 1975, find complete citations for:

(a) The hearings held on February 19 and April 24, 1975.

(b) The committee report on revision of salary fixing procedure for referees.

6. In 1971 and 1972 hearings were held before the Senate Committee on the Judiciary on diversity jurisdiction, multiparty litigation, choice of law in Federal courts and an amended version of the Rules of Civil Procedure for United States District Courts was prepared by the House Committee on the Judiciary. Give complete citations to the hearing and the committee print.

7. (a) Cite the hearing which was held on the preventive detention of criminals in 1970.

   (b) The report of March 25, 1970, by the Committee on the District of Columbia to amend the D.C. Bail Agency Act.

8. Cite the 1970 hearings on the proposal to amend the Constitution to lower the voting age to 18.

9. Give the name of the Commission which compiled a list of the decisions on radiation injuries and workmen's compensation which were issued in 1972.

10. In 1976 Congress reconsidered the Public Works and Economic Development Act and held hearings on the status and implementation of Title 10, Job Opportunities Program. Cite the hearings.

ASSIGNMENT 3
UNITED STATES CODE CONGRESSIONAL AND ADMINISTRATIVE NEWS

Method:

Use index, acts by popular names table, classification and legislative history tables, U.S. Code amendment and repeal tables, etc., in the United States Code Congressional And Administrative News volumes for the 88th Congress, 2nd Session through the 94th Congress, 2nd Session, to locate citations. Include Congress and session in your answers and cite in accordance with the latest edition of A Uniform System Of Citation. State volume and page where answers were located.

Questions:

1. Legislation continues to be introduced in an effort to prevent the tremendous increase in juvenile crime in the hope that this is the key to controlling crime in the United States. It is said that what has been done so far has failed miserably to instill in juveniles any respect for the law through either fear or confidence. Lawyers are paid to get juveniles off just as though they were in adult criminal court and, according to recent newspaper articles, the juvenile court as it is now set up is a standing joke in the juvenile community. Your state is in the process of rewriting its juvenile code and you have been asked to summarize the legislation which led to the Juvenile Delinquency Prevention and Control act of 1968. Cite the following:
   (a) Public Law number and Statutes at Large citation.
   (b) U.S. Code citation.
   (c) Date of approval, House bill number, full names of House and Senate committees reporting, and Congressional Record citation.
   (d) Who did Mr. Javits quote in connection with this legislation?

2. On July 6, 1976, President Ford signed S. 2853 (Pub. L. No. 94-339) to tighten up the accountability of food stamp vendors. On signing the bill, the President expressed disappointment that it was not a major revision of the program and stated that each day that goes by without congressional action to reform the food stamp program costs taxpayers about three million dollars. You have some questions about the integrity of the program. To research the legislation which led to the 1964 Act, cite the following:
   (a) Public Law number of the 1964 Act and the Statutes at Large Citation.
   (b) House bill number, Congress and session. Congressional Record citation. Date House considered passage of the bill, and the name of the committee reporting.
   (c) Find the analysis of the House bill and cite the number of the section dealing with the redemption of coupons.

3. Major legislation was enacted in 1976 to revitalized the nation's railroads, and a new government agency was created to take over the operations of some of the bankrupt Northeast and Midwest railroads. You wish to research the background of the legislation which was enacted in 1973 to

salvage the rail services operated by seven insolvent railroads in the same regions. Cite:

(a) Public Law number of the 1973 Act and the Statutes at Large citation.
(b) United States Code titles which were affected.
(c) Date of approval, House bill number, Committee and Congress, Congressional Record citation.
(d) The names of the four members who stated that, in their view, this legislation wrote into law a detailed collective bargaining agreement negotiated between railway management and labor, and paid for out of the Federal treasury.

4. On July 22, 1975, Attorney General Edward H. Levi presented to the Senate Judiciary Subcommittee on Juvenile Delinquency the Ford Administration's proposed gun control bill, which was intended to correct the flaws in the 1968 Gun Control Act. By September, 1975, the House Judiciary Subcommittee on Crime had 127 bills pending before it and both committees had held extensive hearings on gun control. To research the "flaws" in the 1968 Act find and cite the following:
   (a) Public Law number and Statutes at Large citation.
   (b) United States Code classification for Title I, Secs. 101-105 of the Act.
   (c) The Senate Report, the name of the committee reporting and the Congressional Record citation.
   (d) In Conference Report No. 1956 the title proposed for the Act by the Senate was adopted in lieu of that proposed by the House. Cite the title provided in the House bill.

5. A 1965 study entitled "The Older Worker - Age Discrimination in Employment" was reported by the Secretary of Labor. In 1967 legislation was introduced to correct this, and during Congressional hearings concerning the age limitation witnesses representing airline stewardesses revealed an apparent gross and arbitrary employment distinction based on age alone. To read the history of the 1967 Act cite the following:
   (a) Public Law number and Statutes at Large citation.
   (b) United States Code classification.
   (c) Bill number, Congress, and House committee reporting, Congressional Record citation.
   (d) How many states were cited as having age discrimination legislation of the type proposed in the House bill?

6. The coastal zone management concept which involved some time in the mid-1960s led to the passage of federal legislation in 1972. Under the Act, and subsequent amendments, after a state has adopted a program and has it federally approved, federal actions are to be consistent with that state's program, giving the state additional leverage over federal agency actions. There is a developing legal area that is a major concern of the states, and you wish to evaluate the key issues and incentives in the coastal management program. Cite the following:
   (a) Public Law number of the 1972 Act, Statutes at Large citation.
   (b) United States Code classification.
   (c) Date of approval of the Act. Senate bill number, Congress, and name of Senate Committee reporting, date of passage, Congressional

Record citation.

(d) In his letter to Mr. Magnuson dated April 20, 1970, Mr. Robert R. Keller, Assistant Comptroller General of the United States, suggested a change in the bill regarding the acquisition of real property. What change did he suggest?

7. In his October 1973 anti-inflation message to Congress, President Ford requested new penalties for persons and corporations violating the antitrust laws. A bill to amend the antitrust laws with regard to the conduct of consent decree procedures resulted in legislation in 1974. Cite the following:
   (a) Public Law number and Statutes at Large citation.
   (b) The titles of the United States Code affected.
   (c) The number of the bill introducing the legislation and Congress. Date the House passed the bill and the name of the committee reporting, Congressional Record citation.
   (d) Having found a discussion of the legislation, state name of the person who introduced the first of the three bills relating to Antitrust Procedures and Penalties.

8. Cite the proper title of the 1975 Hazardous Materials Transportation Act, amendment, and Public Law number.

9. Cite the popular title of the provisions enacted under Public Law No. 93-638.

10. Give the Public Law number and the Statutes at Large citation of the legislation which was enacted as a result of H.R. 19,436 in 1970.

ASSIGNMENT 4
COMMERCE CLEARING HOUSE CONGRESSIONAL INDEX

Method:

Use CCH Congressional Index, 1971-1972 (92nd Congress, 1st Session) through 1973-1974 (93rd Congress, 1st Session) to locate authors and number of Congressional bills, companion bills, names of committees to which bills are assigned and committee chairpersons, voting records, status and current status of bills. Cite answers in accordance with the latest edition of A Uniform System Of Citation.

Questions:

1. In the Juvenile Justice and Delinquency Prevention Act of 1974, provisions were made to establish a matching grant program within the Department of Health, Education and Welfare for local and private agencies to develop facilities and programs for runaway youths. A major controversy arose over the decision of who would run the expanded federal aid programs as members of Congress criticized the leadership of LEAA, HEW, and the effectiveness of social service facilities in juvenile delinquency control. Cite:
   (a) The number(s) of the Senate bill(s) which were introduced in connection with the controversy.
   (b) The numbers of any companion or identical bills.
   (c) The House committee(s) to which the first bill listed in a) above was referred.
   (d) The names of the House committees' chairpersons.

2. In 1975 the House reported a bill to amend the Immigration and Nationality Act so as to include a three-step procedure for imposing sanctions against employers who knowingly hire illegal aliens. To compare similar legislation which was passed in 1972, locate the earlier legislation and cite the following:
   (a) The two main sponsors of H.R. 16,188.
   (b) The name of the chairman of the committee to which it was assigned.
   (c) Number of the House report.
   (d) When was the bill sent to the Senate committee?

3. Since the late 1950s there has been agitation for reform of the existing motor vehicle insurance system. In 1974 legislation was proposed which would require all motorists to carry insurance providing compensation for bodily injury regardless of who caused the accident. To check the status of the proposed legislation at the end of the 1st Session of the 93d Congress, find the following:
   (a) The number(s) of the bill(s).
   (b) Numbers of companion or identical bills.
   (c) Who introduced the first bill in (a) above? To which committee was the bill assigned?
   (d) What action had been taken on the bill at the end of 1974?

4. Because of the lack of federal legislation, the only control of surface mining in 1973 rested with the laws enacted by 30 states, and strip mining has inflicted severe damage on the land in Appalachia and the Midwest due to the nation's hunger for power. During the first session in 1973, Congress considered legislation to regulate surface mining of coal. To determine the status of the legislation on land reclamation at the end of the first session, find the following:
   (a) The number(s) of the Senate bill(s).
   (b) Are any companion or identical bills listed?
   (c) The name of the standing House committee to which the Senate bill was referred, and the Senate Report number.
   (d) Date the bill was sent to the President.
   (e) Find a description of the Senate bill and name the sponsor(s).
   (f) How did Senator Mondale vote on the further amendment of October 9, 1973?

5. In April 1972, the Senate had before it a bill to amend the Truth-in-Lending Act of 1968 to protect consumers against unfair billing practices, and to help them resolve credit billing disputes. To determine the outcome of the legislation find the following:
   (a) The number of the Senate bill.
   (b) Are any companion bills listed? Number(s).
   (c) Find a description of the bill, and name the sponsor(s) and the committee to which it was assigned.
   (d) What was the name of the committee chairman?
   (e) Date of passage of the amended bill by the Senate.
   (f) Did Senator Hatfield (R. Or.) vote in favor of the bill?

6. In 1974 Congress found that the prolonged Federal domination of Indian service programs had served to retard rather than enhance the progress of Indian people and their communities by depriving them of the full opportunity to develop leadership skills crucial to the realization of self government, and it has denied them an effective voice in the planning and implementation of programs for their benefit which are responsive to the true needs of Indian communities. That year legislation was introduced to promote maximum Indian participation in the government and education of the Indian people. Cite:
   (a) Number of the bill and Congress.
   (b) Date of Senate hearing. Name of Committee to which the bill was assigned, and the number of the House report.
   (c) Public Law number and the date approved.
   (d) Find a description of the bill and name the sponsor(s).
   (e) Was there a companion bill?
   (f) Name of Senate committee chairperson.

7. One of the most heated issues in Congress in 1972 was the conflict over busing elementary and secondary school children to eliminate racial segregation in education. In 1973 anti-busing constitutional amendments were proposed. To determine the status of the proposed legislation at the end of the first session of the 93d Congress find the following:
   (a) The numbers of the four bills.
   (b) The numbers of the identical bills to the second bill listed above.
   (c) Were any hearings held on the second bill listed in (a) above?

(d) To which committee(s) were the bills assigned?
(e) Who suggested the amendment proposed in the House Joint Resolution of April 1974?

8. During the 92d Congress a companion bill to H. 6978 was introduced in the Senate. Cite the number of the Senate bill and the subject matter of the proposed legislation. Who introduced the Senate bill?

9. Legislation was proposed in H. 1896, 93d Congress, to amend 15 U.S.C. 41 to provide that under certain circumstances exclusive territorial arrangements shall not be deemed unlawful. Give the number of an identical House bill. On which of the two bills was there a hearing? Who introduced the identical bill?

10. On what date was Public Law 92-159 approved? How did Representative Burleson of Texas vote? Give the Congressional Record citation.

ASSIGNMENT 5
CONGRESSIONAL QUARTERLY ALMANAC

Method:

Use table of contents, index, and tables in the Congressional Quarterly Almanac, volumes 28-31, 1972-1975, to research legislative highlights and summaries, bills, dates, congressional committees, presidential statements, voting records. Include volume and page numbers to indicate where the information was found.

Questions:

1. In February 1973, the Senate passed a bill that would provide new procedures to thwart aircraft hijackings. On the same day the United States and Cuba signed an agreement committing each nation to apply penalties to persons convicted of air or sea hijacking. Cite:
   (a) A discussion of the above in which the bill is described.
   (b) How did Senator Schweiker (R. Pa.) vote on the administration's regulations allowing searches?

2. The adverse impact on coastal states of the development of oil and gas resources resulted in the introduction of several bills proposing amendments to the 1953 Act to provide aid to the coastal states affected. Conflicting proposals caused some tension before one of the bills was passed in 1975, and you wish to read a discussion of the legislation. Find the following:
   (a) During the floor action there were complaints that the bill did not include aid to the inland states. What is the number of the bill which was later amended to include some inland states?
   (b) How did Senator Percy (R.Ill.) vote on the proposed amendments to narrow the uses to which states could put these aid funds?

3. In 1976 legislation was introduced to amend the 1972 Marine Mammal Protection Act in order to prohibit the taking of the killer whale, with certain exceptions. The basic thrust of the 1972 Act was to create a moratorium on the taking or importation of marine mammal products, but a controversial exception was given to a specific industry.
   (a) What is the number of the bill which was cleared for the President's signature, and the Public Law number of the Act?
   (b) In the Senate debate of July 25, 1972, on the issue of the moratorium, Harrison A. Williams, Jr. (D. N.J.) offered an amendment to prohibit the Secretary of the Interior or the NOAA Administrator from waiving for a five year period the provision of the moratorium. How did Senator Frank Church (D. Idaho) vote on this amendment?
   (c) Which industry was given the controversial exception?

4. In 1975 legislation was enacted to amend the Sherman Antitrust Act of 1890. There was a Presidential statement in connection with the legislation.
   (a) What was the number of the bill? State the popular name and Public Law number of the Act. What Federal exemptions were repealed?
   (b) During a discussion of the legislation a motion was made to suspend

the rules and pass the bill. What was Representative Udall's position on the motion?

5. In May of 1974 legislation was enacted to amend the Federal Revenue Sharing Act (State and Local Fiscal Assistance Act of 1972). The 1972 legislation provided for revenue sharing initially at an annual rate of $3.5 billion for local governments, and $1.8 billion for state governments, and it created three trust funds. Find a discussion of the 1972 legislation and cite the following:
   (a) The number of the House bill which was approved, and the Public Law number of the Act.
   (b) George Mahon (D. Tex.) made some vigorous comments. How did he vote when the time came for House floor action?

6. In September 1973, a House bill was introduced to amend the Immigration and Nationality Act of 1952, to impose a worldwide limit on United States immigration visas.
   (a) What was the ceiling on visas which the proposed legislation sought to impose?
   (b) How did Henry B. Gonzales (D. Tex.) vote?

7. In December 1975, the United States Senate delayed a final vote on the defense funding bill to discuss the growing controversy regarding American involvement in Angola. An amendment which would have enabled the United States to provide "some assistance resisting Soviet imperialism before it was too late" was rejected although its supporters argued that the Angolan situation was of symbolic importance and that an aid ban would strengthen elements in the Soviet leadership to whom detente was a guise behind which to pursue an expansionist policy without resistance from the United States.
   (a) Cite the names of the two members of Congress who introduced amendments.
   (b) How did Bella S. Abzug vote on the House bill?
   (c) The budget request for Central Intelligence Agency activities was reduced, and the Conference Report was adopted during the second session. State the Public Law number and the Congress.

8. When the Senate Select Committee on Nutrition and Human Needs held hearings in September 1972 on S. 76, which would broaden the definition of "food additives" under the Food, Drug and Cosmetic Act, Dr. John W. Olney of the Washington University School of Medicine, St. Louis, reported on studies of the effects of monosodium glutamate. What did he report?

9. What was the name of the witness representing the Association of the Bar of the City of New York when, on February 5-8, 1973, the House committee addressed the question of whether Congress has the right to enact legislation granting an absolute privilege to newsmen to resist demands for confidential or other unpublished information?

10. Two anti-abortion groups filed lobby registrations during the last two months of 1975. What were the names of the groups and what was each of the lobbyists seeking?

ASSIGNMENT 6
DRILL PROBLEMS

Drill Problem I:

A. Using the array of research tools introduced in the chapter, answer the following. Provide full citations where appropriate.

1. What is the number of the Senate Report on Pub. L. No. 94-427, the Olympic Games Authorization Act of 1976?

2. On June 21, 1977, John J. Duncan made seven pages of testimony to a House subcommittee:
   (a) What bill did the testimony concern?
   (b) What is the CIS fiche code number?
   (c) What is its Superintendent of Documents number?

3. On what date did the Senate consider and pass Pub. L. No. 94-34?

4. What is the Statutes at Large citation for Pub. L. No. 95-209?

5. What does the abbreviation C. P. I. stand for?

B. Using the Index and Daily Digest volumes of the Congressional Record, answer the following for the First Session of the 93rd Congress:

(a) Give the number of two Senate Reports on S-9.
(b) What was the subject of S. 2534?
(c) What legislation was passed in lieu of H.R. 9682?
(d) What was the number of the bill that was enacted as Pub. L. No. 93-222?
(e) What bills were introduced in the Senate on Monday, May 21, 1973?

C. Use the U.S. Code Congressional and Administrative News volumes to answer the following:

1. Using the 1978 U.S.C.C.A.N., answer the following:
   (a) What are the Committee assignments of Congressperson Jack Brinkley?
   (b) Why is there no excerpt printed of the Senate Report on the Presidential Records Act of 1978?

2. Using the 1972 U.S.C.C.A.N., answer the following:
   (a) What were the Committee assignments of Delbert Latta?
   (b) What documents are printed as part of the legislative history of the Equal Employment Opportunity Act of 1972?

3. Using the 1974 U.S.C.C.A.N., answer the following:
   (a) What is the Statutes at Large citation for Pub. L. No. 93-558?
   (b) What reports were made on the Egg Research bill?

D. Use CCH Congressional Index to answer the following:

1. Using the 1975-1976 Congressional Index:
   (a) What was the name of the woman who married Senator Mike Gravel?
   (b) What was the purpose of S. 1298?
   (c) Give the date of a hearing on H.R. 13,950.
   (d) Did Senator Schweiker introduce any bills dealing with the Library of Congress? If so, cite them.
   (e) What is the Committee to which H.R. 11,776 was assigned?

Drill Problem II:

A. Using the array of research tools introduced in the chapter, answer the following. Provide full citations where appropriate.

1. On what date did the President make a statement concerning Pub. L. No. 94-158?

2. On May 17, 1973, Rowland F. Kirks made a statement, and participated in a discussion during hearings on S. 1533.
   (a) What Committee and Subcommittee sponsored the hearings?
   (b) What document was discussed by Mr. Kirks during the hearings?

3. What was the number of the bill that became Pub. L. No. 94-68?

4. On what topic did Professor Shepard Forman testify on June 28, 1977?

5. Find a discussion of the 1974 planned cut in United States aid to the United Nations and the extent of the need for assistance to smaller international organizations. Cite the congressional hearing and CIS Abstract number for the microfiche.

B. Using the Index and Daily Digest volumes of the Congressional Record answer the following:

1. For the First Session of the 91st Congress:
   (a) What bill was the basis of Pub. L. No. 91-54?
   (b) What was the topic of H.R. 12,542?
   (c) What was the final disposition of H.R. 7206?
   (d) On what two subjects did the President submit messages to the Senate on August 6, 1969?
   (e) To what committee was H.R. 9198 referred?
   (f) What was the topic of Senate Joint Resolution 48?

C. Use the <u>U.S. Code Congressional and Administrative News</u> volumes to answer the following:

1. Using the 1978 <u>U.S.C.C.A.N.</u>, answer the following:
   (a) Who is the Chairman of the House Standing Committee on Interstate and Foreign Commerce?
   (b) List the reports that accompanied the Amateur Sports Act of 1978.
2. Using the 1972 <u>U.S.C.C.A.N.</u>, answer the following:
   (a) What was the subject of Presidential Proclamation No. 4169?
   (b) What is the number of the House Conference Report on the Coastal Zone Management Act of 1972?

3. Using the 1974 <u>U.S.C.C.A.N.</u>, answer the following:
   (a) What is the subject of Presidential Proclamation No. 4331?
   (b) Who was the chairman of the Senate Foreign Relations Committee?

D. Use the CCH <u>Congressional Index</u> to answer the following.

1. Using the 1977-1978 <u>Congressional Index</u>:
   (a) Who introduced H.R. 11,774 and to what committee was it referred?
   (b) Give the date of a hearing on H.R. 13662.
   (c) What is the topic of S. 1520?
   (d) On what date did S. 3189 pass the Senate as amended?
   (e) Who was chairman of the Armed Services Committee?

<u>Drill Problem III</u>:

A. Using the array of research tools introduced in the chapter, answer the following. Provide full citations where appropriate.

1. What is the CIS code number for the House Veteran's Affairs Committee?

2. What is the CIS fiche code number for S. Rept. 93-338?

3. What House and Senate committees reported on Pub. L. No. 95-100?

4. What is the CIS fiche number for the Senate Report on Pub. L. No. 95-25?

5. Cite the Public Law number and title of the legislation enacted at the end of 1974, which removed social service programs from their prior close connection with cash public assistance programs, and set up a separate title in the Social Security Act. Where can you read the Presidential statement in connection with this legislation?

B. Using the Index and Daily Digest volumes of the Congressional Record, answer the following.

1. For the First Session of the 92d Congress:
   (a) Give the Senate report number on S. 557.
   (b) What was the subject of H.R. 23?
   (c) How many private bills were enacted into law by this session of Congress?
   (d) What was the number of the bill that was enacted into Pub. L. No. 92-92?
   (e) To which committee was H.R. 248 referred?
   (f) On which page of the Congressional Record would you find an article about "Hoosier Hippies"?

C. Use the U.S. Code Congressional and Administrative News volumes to answer the following.

1. Using the 1978 U.S.C.C.A.N., answer the following:
   (a) Excerpts of what reports are printed as legislative history for Pub. L. No. 95-375?
   (b) On what date did the House finally pass on the Consumer Co-operative Bank Act?

2. Using the 1972 U.S.C.C.A.N., answer the following:
   (a) What is the number of the House Conference Committee report on the Pesticide Control Act? Is it included in U.S.C.C.A.N.?
   (b) What documents are published in U.S.C.C.A.N. as legislative history for the Volunteers in the National Forest Act of 1972?

3. Using the 1974 U.S.C.C.A.N., answer the following:
   (a) What documents are printed in U.S.C.C.A.N. to accompany the Education Amendments of 1974?
   (b) What reports on Pub. L. No. 93-383 are not published in U.S.C.C.A.N.?

D. Using the 1979-1980 Congressional Index:

1. What is Congressman Ron Dellums' birthday?

2. What is the purpose of H.R. 599?

3. What was the date of the House hearing on H.R. 2108?

4. When was Senate Resolution 51 reported without a written report?

5. Who was chairman of the Senate Armed Services Committee's Subcommittee on General Procurement?

CHAPTER 11

STATE AND MUNICIPAL LEGISLATION

ASSIGNMENT 1
STATE LEGISLATION -- GENERAL

Method:

Answer all questions of this assignment using legislative sources for your own state. Cite in accord with the latest edition of A Uniform System of Citation. Cite either specific or illustrative authority as appropriate. Because the questions found in this assignment are cumulative, rather than repetitive, the student should answer each for his/her own jurisdiction.

Questions:

1. Identify the statutory compilation(s) within your jurisdiction.
2. What is the authoritative force of the compilation(s)?
3. Describe the method(s) of supplementation of the compilation(s).
4. Is there a general index to the compilation(s)? Are there separate indexes for individual volumes or titles?
5. What is the most significant difference between the scope of coverage of the general and the separate indexes?
6. Is the index to the compilation(s) arranged typically and factually? Or only typically?
7. Are the references in the general index to compilation sections or to page numbers?
8. In your jurisdiction is there an overall index to general, special, local and temporary acts which are not included in the statutory compilation(s)?
9. How, if at all, are cases construing provisions of the compilation(s) located?
10. Does the compilation(s) include references or citations to opinions of the state attorney general? If so, where are they found?
11. Indicate the cross references, if any, to other non-statutory research aids found in the compilation(s).
12. Does the compilation(s) contain textual commentaries or general historical essays?

13. Describe the historical notes, if any, given for each section of the compilation(s).

14. Are there cross references to related sections of the compilation(s)? Where are they found?

15. Are cross references to comparable legislation in other jurisdictions given in the compilation(s)? If not, locate a compilation containing such cross references.

16. Is the effective date of each section of the compilation(s) given? If not, what date is given? Where would one find the effective date?

17. Is there a separate table of acts by popular names? If not how are acts by popular names indexed?

18. Are there parallel references from earlier compilations to the present? Where are they located? If not, how does one trace from a prior compilation to a current compilation?

19. Is there a reference table from the session laws of the state to the compilation(s)? Where is the table located?

20. Does the index to your state constitution contain specific terms leading you directly to cases construing the constitution?

21. Describe the general procedure to be followed in locating specific cases construing a provision of your state constitution.

22. Locate and cite the "due process" clause of your state constitution.

23. Under the constitution of your state, can a minor traffic violation be used as justification to search the car of a defendant without a search warrant?

24. Does your state compilation(s) include the United States Constitution? If yes, is it annotated? Where is it located?

25. Does your state have a formalized procedure for advising one of pending legislation? If so, describe it.

ASSIGNMENT 2
STATE CODES--USE OF INDEXES

Method:

Using the index to the latest code of your state, locate the current statutory laws on the following subjects:

Questions:

1. Arbitration laws.
2. Pollution laws.
3. Powers of attorney laws.
4. Landlord and tenant laws.
5. Specific performance laws.
6. Chiropractors laws.
7. Fictitious name laws.
8. Franchise laws.
9. Gambling laws.
10. Gifts to minors laws.
11. Descent and distribution laws.
12. Extradition laws.
13. Fraud laws.
14. Hunting laws.
15. Insolvency laws.
16. Municipal corporations laws.
17. Drug laws.
18. Mechanics' liens laws.
19. Trademarks and tradenames laws.
20. Trust companies laws.
21. Attachment laws.

Chapter 11

22. Housing laws.

23. Workmen's compensation laws.

24. Birth certificates laws.

25. Nursing homes laws.

26. Capital punishment, existence of .

27. Next of kin, who is?

28. Homicide, definition of.

29. Homestead exemptions.

30. Legislation governing use of state flag.

ASSIGNMENT 3
STATE CODES -- CONSTRUCTION

Method:

Using bound volumes, bound supplements, specific pamphlet supplements, pocket parts, general pamphlet supplements, the tables of statutes construed from the appropriate reporter bound volumes and advance sheets, cite the most recent case construing each statutes located in Assignment 2.

ASSIGNMENT 4
STATE CODES -- DERIVATION

Method:

Using the same sources employed in Assignment 2, locate and cite the oldest legislation noted as part of the history of each of the statutes found as a result thereof. Cite in accord with the latest edition of A Uniform System of Citation.

ASSIGNMENT 5
STATE SESSION LAWS -- PARALLEL REFERENCE TABLES

Method:

Using parallel reference tables from the appropriate state codes, convert the following citations to their current equivalent.

Questions:

1. 1935 Del. Code sec. 575.
2. 1863 Ga. Code sec. 3796.
3. 1955 Hawaii Rev. Laws sec. 30-9.
4. 1919 Ida. Comp. Stat. sec. 3201.
5. 1874 Ill. Rev. Stat. c. 34, p. 302, sec. 67.
6. 1954 Maine Rev. Stat. c. 144, sec. 7.
7. 1930 Miss. Code sec. 4941.
8. 1942 N. H. Rev. Laws sec. 229:71.
9. 1929 N. Mex. Comp. Stat. sec. 4-2103.
10. 1910 Okla. Rev. Laws sec. 7381.

ASSIGNMENT 6
STATE CODES -- COMPARATIVE RESEARCH

Sources: Model Business Corporation Act Annotated (3d ed. 1985).

Martindale-Hubbell Law Directory (1990).

Book of the States, 1988-89 (1988).

Method:

Using the sources listed above, answer the following questions. When required, cite sources in accord with the latest edition A Uniform System of Citation.

Questions:

A. Use the Model Business Corporation Act Annotated, 3d.

1. Locate and cite the section on voluntary dissolution by act of the corporation. Is this model act provision identical or comparable with that of your state? If so, cite your state's statute.

2. Locate and cite the appropriate section on failure of the corporation to hold annual meetings. Does any state have a provision identical in substance with this section? If so, cite that state's statute.

3. Locate the section dealing with payment of cash dividends; indicate whether the Model Act provision is identical with that of your state.

4. What is the minimum number of directors required for a corporation? What do the corporation laws of your home state and the states contiguous thereto require?

B. Use Martindale-Hubbell Law Directory (1990). For each answer, give the subject heading(s) under which the answer was found, the jurisdictions, and the authority specified in Martindale-Hubbell. Give answers for Alabama, Louisiana and Mississippi.

1. Age of majority.

2. Time specified by statute of limitations to recover damages for wrongful death.

3. Drug use as a ground for divorce.

4. Seat of the supreme court, i.e., highest court of appeal.

C. Use <u>Book of the States</u> 1988-89 (1988). For all answers, give the page on which the answers were found.

1. Identify the states having the highest and lowest individual income tax rates. Specify the rates.

2. What is the method of selecting Supreme Court Justices in Louisiana, Alabama and Mississippi?

3. Using the Book of the States 1988-89, which state had the largest number of measures vetoed by the governor?

ASSIGNMENT 7
MARTINDALE-HUBBELL LAW DIRECTORY - FOREIGN LAW DIGESTS

Method:

Using the summaries of foreign legislation in the Law Digests volume of the Martindale-Hubbell Law Directory, ascertain whether alcoholism or drunkenness constitute grounds for either a divorce or a separation in the following countries:

1. Argentina
2. Australia
3. Columbia
4. Costa Rica
5. El Salvador
6. Guatemala
7. Ireland (Eire)
8. Italy
9. Mexico
10. Venezuela

ASSIGNMENT 8
MUNICIPAL CODES

Method:

Refer to the municipal code of the city in which your law school is located, or the one for your home town, or one that is readily available in the law library that you are using. Identify the code that you select for its exercise. Explain briefly the provisions of the ordinance as called for below and include a citation to the pertinent provision.

Question:

1. Is there an ordinance relating to false or misleading advertising?

2. Is there an air pollution ordinance?

3. Is there an ordinance regulating door to door solicitors and vendors?

4. Is there an ordinance regulating the size of signs that may be used by merchants?

5. Is there an ordinance on drunk driving?

6. Is there an ordinance relating to false arrest?

7. Is there an ordinance on littering the streets?

8. Is there an ordinance relating to loitering near election polls on election days?

9. Is there an ordinance prohibiting pinball machines?

10. Is loud noise near hospitals prohibited by ordinance?

11. Is there an ordinance on consumption of alcoholic beverages in motor vehicles?

12. Is there a curfew ordinance for minors?

13. Does an ordinance give pedestrians the right of way at crosswalks?

14. Is there an ordinance relating to reckless driving?

15. Is there an ordinance relating to stealing or removing vehicle parts or accessories?

ASSIGNMENT 9
DRILL PROBLEMS

Drill Problem I:

Locate the following:

1. The code section designating the Cherokee rose as Georgia's State Floral Emblem.

2. The Hawaii Code section defining the rights of a buyer of a horse or mule with glandus.

3. The Idaho Code section giving corporations the authority to issue no-par stock.

4. The current state code cites for the following:

   (a) 1965 Ill. Laws 1400 § 1.
   (b) 1935 Ind. Acts Ch. 128 § 1.
   (c) 1927 Iowa Code § 13615.
   (d) Ky. Carroll's Civ. Code § 460.

Drill Problem II:

Locate the following:

1. The section of the Maryland code requiring the clerks of county courts to endorse each deed to real property.

2. The section of the Massachusetts code providing for a lower than normal minimum wage for theatrical ushers.

3. The section of the Michigan code providing for a study of sand dunes within the state.

4. The current state code cites for the following:

   (a) 1969 Minn. Laws Ch. 895 § 1.
   (b) 1972 Mo. Laws, p. 605 § 1.
   (c) 1942 Miss. Code § 1186.
   (d) 1979 N.H. Laws Ch. 492 § 1.

CHAPTER 12

COURT RULES AND PROCEDURES

ASSIGNMENT 1
FEDERAL RULES OF CIVIL PROCEDURE

Sources:

Title 28 United States Code Annotated or United States Code Service covering 1-86 of the Federal Rules of Civil Procedure.

C. Wright and A. Miller, Federal Practice and Procedure covering Federal Rules of Civil Procedure.

J. Moore, Moore's Federal Practice (2d ed.) covering Federal Rules of Civil Procedure.

Method:

Briefly answer the questions. Cite to rule numbers, treatises and cases as required. Use any of the sources listed above.

Questions:

1. Cite the section in Moore which discusses the Supreme Court's authority to promulgate rules of procedure under the Rule-Making Statute of 1934.

2. In what years have subdivisions (b), (d)(4), (d)(7), (e), and (f) of Rule 4 been changed.

3. What rule prescribes a uniform method of service upon the United States in all actions governed by the Federal Rules?

4. Cite the rule which indicates if it is a requirement that the signing of pleadings must always be verified or accompanied by an affidavit.

5. In what year was Rule 6(c) rescinded? Why was this rule rendered unnecessary?

6. Cite the rule regarding depositions pending appeal.

7. Using Wright and Miller, cite a 1958 6th Circuit case in which a bank sought a declaratory judgment that it would be unlawful for a state bank to open a branch in the same city. Cite also the section in Wright and Miller under which the case is cited.

8. If a court orders separate trials as provided in rule 42(b), judgment on a counterclaim or cross-claim may be rendered in accordance with what rule?

9. Rule 14 was modeled on what Admirality Rule?

10. Rule 23(a) is a substantial restatement of what earlier Equity Rule?

11. Under the Federal Rules, does the court have the power to order a summary judgment without a hearing? Cite applicable rules and section in Wright and Miller.

12. Is shareholder-plaintiff in a successful derivative action entitled to reimbursement of attorney's fees? Cite applicable section in Wright and Miller.

13. Upon motion, the court may order that testimony taken at disposition be recorded by other than stenographic means. If so, should the order designate the manner of recording? Cite rule number.

14. Rule 4 remained as promulgated in 1937 until 1963. What subdivision(s) of this rule still remain unchanged?

15. Has Rule 47(b) ever been revised? If so, what was the effective date of the latest revision?

Chapter 12

ASSIGNMENT 2
FEDERAL RULES OF CRIMINAL PROCEDURE

Sources: Title 18 United States Code Annotated or United States Code Service covering Rules 1-60 of the Federal Rules of Criminal Procedure.

C. Wright and A. Miller, Federal Practice and Procedure covering the Federal Rules of Criminal Procedure.

J. Moore, Moore's Federal Practice (2d ed.) covering the Federal Rules of Criminal Procedure.

Method:

Briefly answer the questions. Cite to rule numbers, treatises and cases as required. Use any of the sources listed above.

Questions:

1. When used in the Federal Rules of Criminal Procedure, does the word "state" include the District of Columbia? Cite applicable rule.

2. May a defendant waive his right to preliminary examination? Cite applicable rule.

3. Is it proper for an attorney for the government to challenge a grand juror after the oath to the grand juror has been administered? Cite pertinent rule.

4. Must a motion raising defenses and objections based on defects in the institution of the prosecution always be made before trial? Cite pertinent rule.

5. Are statements made by accused in psychiatric examination admissible as evidence against the accused on the issue of guilt? Cite rule.

6. According to United States v. Anzelmo, is the record of prior criminal convictions of persons whom government intends to call as witnesses at trial discovered under Rule 16?

7. Rule 17(f) of the Federal Rules of Criminal Procedure is substantially the same as what rule of the Federal Rules of Civil Procedure?

8. Cite a rule which indicates if the indigent defendant in a criminal case has the right to secure attendance of witnesses at

the expense fo the Government.

9. When did the rule establishing a basis for pretrial conferences with counsel for the parties in criminal cases become effective? Cite pertinent rule.

10. Under what circumstances may a jury consist of less than twelve persons? Cite pertinent rule.

11. If a judge presiding over a case dies prior to sentencing, must the successor judge always order a new trial? Cite pertinent rule.

12. A motion for a new trial based on grounds other than newly discovered evidence must normally be made within how many days of a verdict? Cite pertinent rule.

13. What rule gives a court discretion in deciding whether to stay an order placing a defendant on probation?

14. Who may request that a search warrant be issued? Cite pertinent rule.

15. If a judge certifies that he actually saw or heard conduct constituting contempt being committed in the actual presence of the court, is it necessary for the contempt to be prosecuted on notice? Cite pertinent rules.

Chapter 12

ASSIGNMENT 3
USE OF FEDERAL PROCEDURE FORMS

Sources: West's Federal Forms.

Federal Procedural Forms (Lawyers Edition).

C. Wright and A. Miller, Federal Practice and Procedure, volume 3, appendix.

Method:

Using the source indicated, locate forms, citing volume number, page number, and section number, when applicable.

Questions:

A. Use West's Federal Forms:

1. An order granting motion for summary judgment and dismissing motion for preliminary injunction.

2. Claim of owner to articles seized under Food and Drug Act.

3. Order for writ of habeas corpus.

4. A pre-trial order in a railroad crossing accident case.

5. A jury instruction on alibi.

B. Use Federal Procedural Forms (Lawyers Edition):

1. Form for attorney affidavit in support of a motion for new trial.

2. Complaint for common law trademark infringement for use of plaintiff's corporate name.

3. Motion for new trial in action tried by jury.

4. Order for discharge of a trustee in bankruptcy.

5. Motion in Supreme Court to dismiss an appeal for lack of jurisdiction.

C. Use C. Wright and A. Miller Federal Practice and Procedure, volume 3, appendix:

1. Cite form number for motion in arrest of judgment.

2. Cite form number for warrant for arrest of witness.
3. Cite form number to be used in connection with bail bond or appearance bond.
4. Cite form number for an indictment for murder in the first degree of a federal officer.
5. Cite form number for motion for new trial.

ASSIGNMENT 4
COURT RULES

Method:

Use the court rules volumes of United State Code Annotated (USCA) and/or United States Code Service (USCS) to answer the following questions, citing the rule number:

Questions:

1. Under the Federal Rules of Appellate Procedure, is leave or consent required for a state to file an amicus curiae brief?

2. Unless the Court has provided otherwise, at what time is the appendix to a brief to be filed in a United States Court of Appeals?

3. May anyone remove books from the Supreme Court Library?

4. In the Supreme Court, how much time is usually allowed for oral argument?

5. Before the Supreme Court will admit an attorney applying to practice in the Court, she/he must have been admitted to practice in the highest court of a state, etc., for how long?

6. What rule provides for law students to appear in the United States Court of Appeals for the District of Columbia?

ASSIGNMENT 5
WRIGHT'S FEDERAL PRACTICE AND PROCEDURE

Method:

Using C. Wright and A. Miller, Federal Practice and Procedure, answer the following questions, giving citations where necessary.

Questions:

1. What 1952 Supreme Court case upheld the admissibility of evidence obtained through use of a "wired" undercover agent in a criminal case?

2. Where is there discussion of the meaning of the word "admissible" as used in Rule 402 of the Federal Rules of Evidence?

3. Where are the implications of "negative pregnants" in the Federal Rules of Civil Procedure discussed?

4. Where can one find the forms mentioned in Rule 84 of Federal Rules of Civil Procedure?

5. Which of the Federal Rules of Criminal Procedure gave government a right to discovery against criminal defendants for the first time?

6. Where is there discussion of pretrial conferences in complex cases?

7. May an injunction be binding on unnamed members of a labor union?

8. Where is there a discussion of Ex parte Young as it relates to relations of state and federal courts?

9. Where is there a discussion of the law controlling the question of immunity from service of process?

ASSIGNMENT 6
MOORE'S FEDERAL PRACTICE

Method:

Using J. Moore, Moore's Federal Practice (2d ed.), answer the questions, giving citations as necessary.

Questions:

1. Which court has original jurisdiction in federal question suits brought by Indian tribes?

2. Is an injunction subject to collateral attack?

3. After remand, may a trial court correct an error existing but not raised on an interlocutory appeal?

4. Does one have a permissive right to intervene in a claim or defense when such claim or defense has a question of law or fact in common with the main action?

5. Applying conflict of law rules in non-federal matters, must state substantive law be applied?

6. Can a party's deposition be used as original evidence and also for impeachment purposes if being used by an adverse party?

7. May a third-party defendant assert a counterclaim against a plaintiff?

8. At which paragraph is waiver by defendant of right to remove discussed?

9. The "final judgment rule" as to the appealability of any decree other than one that is a final judgment is a complex one. Where can one find some illuminating discussion of the general rule?

10. Where can one find discussion of the general history that surrounds Rule 62 of the Federal Rules of Civil Procedure?

ASSIGNMENT 7
WEINSTEIN'S EVIDENCE

Method:

Using J. Weinstein & M. Berger, Weinstein's Evidence, answer the following questions, giving citations where necessary.

Questions:

1. Where is there discussion of the degree of privilege that attaches to communications in a group therapy setting?

2. Where is Burr v. Kase noted?

3. Where can one find discussion of the right of a judge to comment on the credibility of witnesses?

4. Where can one find discussion of admissibility of ballistic expert testimony linking defendant to the weapon used in a crime?

5. Where is Polen's "The Admissibility of Truth Serum Tests in Court" cited?

6. Where is Connecticut General Statute §1443i mentioned in the text?

7. Where is the proper form of an offer of proof discussed?

CHAPTER 13

ADMINISTRATIVE LAW

ASSIGNMENT
USE OF THE CODE OF FEDERAL REGULATIONS

Sources: C.F.R. Index and Finding Aids
Bowker Code of Federal Regulations Index
CIS Index to the Code of Federal Regulations

Method:

Using any of the available indexes to the C.F.R., locate and cite the appropriate title and section for each of the following problems:

Questions:

1. Where in the C.F.R. is it specifically stated that it is an unlawful employment practice to classify a job as "male" or "female" or to maintain separate lines of progression or separate seniority lists based on sex where this would adversely affect any employee unless sex is a bona fide occupational qualification for the job?

2. In which C.F.R. title and section does the Occupational Safety and Health Administration of the Department of Labor specify the amount of airborne concentrations of asbestos fibers to which an employee may be exposed in an eight hour period?

3. Under which C.F.R. title and part is the procedure for reporting natural gas pipeline leaks given?

4. What C.F.R. title and section governs the withholding of U.S. Government checks which are intended for delivery in certain countries where it has been determined that postal, transportation, or banking facilities are such that there is not a reasonable assurance that named payees in those areas will actually receive these checks and be able to negotiate them for full value?

5. What C.F.R. title and part is intended to effectuate the provisions of a portion of the Civil Rights Act of 1964 requiring equal employment opportunities in all programs or activities receiving Federal financial assistance from the U.S. Coast Guard?

6. Where in the C.F.R. is the provision establishing a maximum liability of fifty dollars per card for credit card holders in cases involving unauthorized use of such cards?

7. Where in the C.F.R. is it specified that misuse of the word "perfect" in describing a diamond is an unfair trade practice?

8. Where in the C.F.R. is the description of the signaling arrangements, i.e., the attention signal, whereby standard, FM, and television broadcast stations can actuate muted receivers for the receipt of cuing announcements as part of the Emergency Broadcast System?

9. Where in the C.F.R. are the provisions which deal with the "Warnings" which packages of antacid products for human use must carry to avoid being misbranded?

10. Where in the C.F.R. are the reporting requirements for accidents involving the transportation of radioactive materials?

11. The Postal regulations provide that the Domestic Mail Manual is available for reference and inspection at various places including all U.S. Post Offices and branches. What portion thereof deals with Postage Meters and Meter Stamps?

12. Where in the C.F.R. is the provision governing the use of non-federal funds in federally sponsored vocational rehabilitation programs for the mentally retarded?

13. Where in the C.F.R. are the federal grade standards for frozen okra enumerated?

14. Where in the C.F.R. are the provisions as authorized by the Federal Truth in Lending Act which govern the determination of finance charges?

15. Where in the C.F.R. are the provisions covering the labeling requirements for "Lemon Juice?"

16. Where in the C.F.R. are the provisions governing the service of process and subpoenas upon personnel of the Department of the Navy?

17. Where in the Domestic Mail Manual are the provisions governing commemorative stamps?

18. Where in the Domestic Mail Manual are the provisions specifying what may be mailed?

19. Where in the C.F.R. are the provisions of the Social Security Administration covering insurance benefits for victims of black lung disease?

20. Where in the C.F.R. are the provisions of the Food and Drug Administration specifying the standard of fill for a container of canned applesauce?

21. Where in the C.F.R. are there provisions dealing with the rate of import tax on beer as of the time of its importation, or, if entered into customs custody, at the time of removal from such custody?

22. 42 U.S.C. §263 is the federal law authorizing the U.S. Public Health Service to prepare certain biological products when not available from licensed establishments. Cite C.F.R. parts issued under this statute as shown in the C.F.R. Index and Finding Aids.

23. Pollution of navigable waters by the discharge of oil of all types is covered by what title and part of the C.F.R.? Set out the U.S. Code reference cited as authority for this part.

24. Locate the C.F.R. definition of "cable television system."

25. Cite the C.F.R. part covering the labeling or advertising of automobile tires.

26. Federal flood insurance regulations define the coverage of this insurance. Are mud slides covered? Cite the definition regulation for this.

27. Any person may bring to the attention of the Civil Rights Commission a grievance believed to fall within its jurisdiction. Should the complaint include the names and titles of the officials or other persons involved in acts forming the basis for the complaint?

28. There are quarantine regulations which the U.S. Surgeon General administers. Cite the regulation which lists the various diseases that are "Quarantinable."

29. Find the policy forms used by the Federal Crime Insurance Program and give the citation for the required Commercial Crime Insurance Policy form.

30. Are consular or other foreign service officers permitted to celebrate marriages? What regulation covers the consular office acting as an official witness to a marriage?

CHAPTER 14

LOOSELEAF SERVICES

ASSIGNMENT 1
USE OF LOOSE-LEAF SERVICES OR REPORTERS

Method:

Briefly answer the question and give the citation requested using the form required by the latest edition of A Uniform System of Citation to the extent that the indicated source provides the information needed for such a citation.

Questions:

1. Source: C.C.H. Standard Federal Tax Reporter. Where a taxpayer does not establish a basis for measuring an alleged casualty loss of ornamental trees, will a deduction be allowed? Cite the C.C.H. paragraph on point.

2. Source: C.C.H. Standard Federal Tax Reporter. Was a newspaper subscriber taxable on the value of an automobile which he won on a lottery ticket received with his subscription as part of a campaign by the newspaper to increase its circulation? Cite a case on point.

3. Source: C.C.H. Standard Federal Tax Reporter. May a member of the U.S. foreign service, i.e., a consular officer, take a business traveling expense deduction for transportation, meals, and lodging that is occasioned by being on "home leave?" Cite a Revenue Ruling on point.

4. Source: C.C.H. Standard Federal Tax Reporter. May letter carriers deduct the cost and maintenance expenses of uniforms? Cite a Revenue Ruling on point.

5. Source: C.C.H. Standard Federal Tax Reporter. Is the amount of a dissolved partnership debt paid by a former partner on behalf of a deceased partner's insolvent estate deductible? Cite a Revenue Ruling on point.

6. Source: C.C.H. Standard Federal Tax Reporter. In some cases may the cost of improvements made by business tenants in lieu of paying rent be deductible as rent? Cite the C.C.H. paragraph on point.

7. Source: C.C.H. Standard Federal Tax Reporter. Are travel expenses of teachers on sabbatical leave deductible if and to the extent that the travel is directly related to the duties of the teacher in his teaching position? Cite a Revenue Ruling on point.

8. Source: C.C.H. <u>Standard Federal Tax Reporter</u>. Were the legal fees incurred in an unsuccessful attempt to have a liquor license transferred from one bar to another building which the taxpayer owned deductible? Cite a case on point.

9. Source: C.C.H. <u>Standard Federal Tax Reporter</u>. Is a monthly charge or "tax" made by a city for the use of its sewer system a deductible personal expense as are property taxes? Cite the C.C.H. paragraph on point.

10. Source: P-H <u>Federal Taxes</u>. Are penalties paid by truck operators for violations of state size and weight limit laws deductible business expenses? Cite the P-H paragraph on point.

11. Source: P-H <u>Federal Taxes</u>. What is the Federal income tax status of subsistence and uniform allowances that are granted to personnel of the Public Health Service of the United States? Cite the pertinent section of the Income Tax Regulations.

12. Source: P-H <u>Federal Taxes</u>. Was the cost of restoring a part of a trellis which collapsed on a hop ranch as a result of an extraordinarily large crop, rainfall, and wind deductible as a business expenses? Cite a Board of Tax Appeals decision on point.

13. Source: P-H <u>Federal Taxes</u>. Where the taxpayer alleged in his complaint that but for the patent infringement asserted he would have been in receipt of large gains and profits, was the entire amount of damages received held to be income for purposes of taxation? Cite a First Circuit case on point.

14. Source: C.C.H. <u>Federal Securities Law Reporter</u>. Where the defendant wrote a letter to a woman purchaser of securities he was selling and stated, "if you know of some of your friends whom you can write to and simply state that if they still want some of it (interest in an electrical device represented to extract gold from water) you can get them some for a few days. .." Was this construed as evidence to show that the defendant was offering units of interest to the general public? Cite a case on point.

15. Source: C.C.H. <u>Federal Securities Law Reporter</u>. Did a Federal District Court have jurisdiction to hear a case in which a stockholder sought enforcement of the proxy solicitation rules promulgated under section 14 of the Securities Exchange Act of 1934 notwithstanding the fact that the Securities and Exchange Commission had declined to institute a court action against the defendant for such purpose. Cite a case on point.

16. Source: C.C.H. <u>Federal Securities Law Reporter</u>. Did a bank which credited the account of a customer upon having endorsed to it the customer's draft on a third party, accompanied by a spurious warehouse receipt securing a like note, in subsequently receiving payment from the third party, effect a sale within the meaning of section 2(3) of the Securities Act? Cite a Third Circuit case on point.

17. Source: C.C.H. Standard Federal Tax Reporter. Are legal expenses deductible where incurred by a husband in resisting his wife's suit for divorce deductible as such? Cite the U.S. Sup. Ct. cases on point.

18. Source: C.C.H. Standard Federal Tax Reporter. Does the operation of a dining room, cafeteria, and snack bar by an exempt art museum for the use of its employees and members of the visiting public constitute an unrelated business activity? Cite the pertinent Revenue Ruling so determining.

19. Source: C.C.H. Standard Federal Tax Reporter. A stock purchase plan for an employee allowed him to buy stock with a current market value of $100 by paying only $85 per share for it. Will he be taxable on the $15 difference in value at the time he purchases this stock? What section of the Int. Rev. Code applies here?

20. Source: C.C.H. Standard Federal Tax Reporter. X is enrolled as a student in a recognized educational institution taking a full time day course for only five calendar months during 1972. Does this limited enrollment fit the definition of a "student" so that his parents may use him as a personal exemption? Cite regulation shown.

21. Source: C.C.H. Consumer Credit Guide. Under "Charts" section find Home Solicitation Sales. Are insurance sales excluded from statutes giving buyers right to cancel within time limitations shown in the states of Florida, Michigan and Wisconsin?

22. Source: C.C.H. Consumer Credit Guide. What is the maximum liability that a credit card holder can incur under the Federal Reserve Board regulations with respect to the "unauthorized use" of his credit card? Give Federal Reserve Board regulation citation.

23. Source: C.C.H. Consumer Credit Guide. Find the Federal Reserve Board Regulation Z under Federal-Truth-In-Lending. Under what regulation section can you find a definition of "open end credit?"

24. Source: C.C.H. Poverty Law Reporter. Does section 514 of the Soldiers' and Sailors' Civil Relief Act entitle service men stationed in Connecticut but regularly domiciled and resident elsewhere to exemption from the payment of Connecticut sales and use taxes? Cite C.C.H. paragraph on point.

ASSIGNMENT 2
USE OF LOOSE-LEAF SERVICE CITATORS

Method:

Answer the question by giving the citator reference as shown or otherwise providing the information requested.

Questions:

1. Source: C.C.H. Standard Federal Tax Reporter Citator. The Las Vegas Land Water Co. case. 26 T.C. 881. was cited in a later opinion of the Tax Court. What is the Tax Court Reports citation for the citing case?

2. Source: C.C.H. Standard Federal Tax Reporter Citator. The case of Phillips v. Howe Films Co. was first decided by a Federal District Court for Pennsylvania. Was this decision affirmed or reversed by the Third Circuit?

3. Source: P-H Federal Taxes Citator, 2d Series, vol. 1. Income Tax Unit Ruling 3064, 1937-1 C.B. 94, was questioned in what case?

4. Source: P-H Federal Taxes Citator (Loose-leaf). The case of David v. Phinney, 16 A.F.T.R. 2d 5290, has been cited by two later cases for the topic of law which is treated in the first paragraph of the syllabus to the cited case. What are these cases?

5. Source: C.C.H. Federal Estate and Gift Tax Reporter, vol. 3. You are looking for the case involving the Estate of Frank Janson. What part of the official citation can be developed from the citator?

6. Source: C.C.H. Standard Federal Tax Reporter Citator. Which federal courts heard the case of Rose E. Roybark?

7. Source: C.C.H. Standard Federal Tax Reporter Citator. Did the Commissioner of Internal Revenue indicate acquiesce in the holding of the Tax Court in the case involving Lola G. Bullard, 5 T.C. 1346? In what volume of the Cumulative Bulletin is the Commissioner's action reported?

8. Source: C.C.H. Standard Federal Tax Reporter Citator. The United States Court of Appeals affirmed the Tax Court in the case involving William E. Conroy. Did the action of the Court of Appeals appear in a full opinion or a per curiam opinion?

9. Source: P-H Federal Taxes Citator, 2d Series, vol. 1. The same case as was involved in Department of Labor Release, 9-6-56, 1956 P-H para. 76,702, was also involved in what Revenue Ruling?

10. Source: C.C.H. Federal Estate and Gift Tax Reporter, vol. 3. The case of Leonard D. Reeves, Admr. (Est. of T.K. Reeves) v. U.S., 57-2 U.S.T.C. para. 11,717, was cited in what 1971 Revenue Ruling?

11. Source: C.C.H. Standard Federal Tax Reporter Citator. Did the U.S. Court of Appeals for the Sixth Circuit reverse or affirm the Tax Court in the case involving George L. Sogg?

12. Source: C.C.H. Standard Federal Tax Reporter Citator. Who appealed the decision of the United States Board of Tax Appeals to the U.S. Court of Appeals in the case involving Little Gem Coal Company?

13. Source: P-H Federal Tax Service Citator, vol. 3. What is the American Federal Tax Reports citation for the opinion which reversed the Jerry Rossman Corp. case, 10 T.C. 468?

14. Source: C.C.H. Federal Estate and Gift Tax Reporter Citator. What is the citation for the Snyder case which cited Worcester County Trust Co. (Est. of E.E. Aldrich) v. U.S.?

15. Source: P-H Federal Taxes Citator, 2d Series, vol. 1. Revenue Ruling 59-277 was reversed by what later Revenue Ruling?

16. Source: P-H Federal Taxes Citator, 2d Series, vol. 1. Revenue Ruling 67-282 revoked what earlier Revenue Ruling?

17. Source: P-H Federal Taxes Citator, 2d Series, vol. 1. Revenue Ruling 59-60 was modified by what later ruling?

18. Source: P-H Federal Taxes Citator, 2d Series, vol. 1. I.T. 2143, IV-1 CB 214 was superseded by what Revenue Ruling?

19. Source: P-H Federal Taxes Citator, 2d Series, vol. 1. The William G. Lias case (24 T.C. 280) was affirmed by what decision of the federal appellate court?

20. Source: P-H Federal Taxes Citator 2d Series, vol 1. The Tax Court case involving Joseph L. Merrill, 9 T.C. 291, was followed in what later Tax Court memo?

21. Source: P-H Federal Taxes Citator, vol. 1. Headnote No. 3 of Guettel v. U.S., 95 F.2d 229, was followed by what case?

22. Source: P-H Federal Taxes Citator, vol. 1. Shellabarger, Maud Dunlap v. Commissioner, 14 B.T.A. 695, was reversed by what appellate decision?

23. Source: P-H Federal Taxes Citator, vol. 1. What did Richmond Hosiery Mills v. Commissioner, 29 F. 2d. 262, do to the Richmond Hosiery Mills case, 6 B.T.A. 1247?

24. Source: P-H Federal Taxes Citator, vol. 1. What did I.T. 2968 do to I.T. 2472?

25. Source: P-H Federal Taxes Citator, vol. 1. T.D. 3911 was cited in a U.S. Supreme Court case. Give this citation without date.

26. Source: P-H Federal Taxes Citator, vol. 1. General Counsel's Memorandum 6667 was modified by a latter G.C.M. Cite the latter.

27. Source: Pike and Fischer Radio Regulation Finding Aids Volume. Give the first citation of 27 F.C.C.2d 743 that appears in 45 R.R. 2d.

28. Source: Pike and Fischer Radio Regulation Finding Aids Volume. The Fairness Doctrine Rules appeared in 10 R.R.2d 1901. Find the last citation to these rules that appears in 24 R.R.2d.

29. Source: C.C.H. Standard Federal Tax Reporter Citator. Did the Commissioner acquiesce in the Tax Court decision involving John F. Lewis, Jr.? Give as shown the action of the Third Circuit Court of Appeals in this case.

30. Source: C.C.H. Standard Federal Tax Reporter Citator. The Court of Appeals decision of Mrs. Leonie G. Mayer v. Donnelly was cited in a later decision, the Swenson case. What is the citation of such Swenson decision?

31. Source: C.C.H. Standard Federal Tax Reporter Citator. Did the U.S. Supreme Court grant certiorari in the Francis Doll case? The Eighth Circuit Doll opinion was cited in Northwest Security National Bank. Give the citator reference to this latter decision as shown.

32. Source: C.C.H. Standard Federal Tax Reporter at Case Table. Was the District Court decision in Ralph M. Currie, Jr. v. Internal Revenue Service affirmed by the Court of Appeals for the 11th Circuit? Give the U.S.T.C. citation for this latter decision.

33. Source: C.C.H. Federal Estate & Gift Tax Reporter Citator. Give as shown the Tax Court citation to the Estate of Mary H. Hays v. Commissioner. What did the Fifth Circuit, Court of Appeals do to the original Tax Court decision?

34. Source: C.C.H. Federal Estate & Gift Tax Reporter Citator. The case of Estate of Carrie Grossman, was decided by the Tax Court. Give the volume and page citation as shown for this decision. Cite also the 1970 Revenue Ruling which later referred to this Grossman decision.

35. Source: C.C.H. Federal Estate & Gift Tax Reporter Citator. Give as shown the citation to the Court of Claims case, Stewart P. Verckler, Exr (Estate of M.S. Verckler) v. U.S. In 1962 the Lorenz case in the Court of Appeals cited the Verckler decision. How was this reference to the Lorenz case set out in the citator?

ASSIGNMENT 3
THEME PROBLEMS AND DRILL PROBLEMS

Theme Problem I:

Many of the cases on discrimination that followed the Brown decision related to discrimination in labor. One of the most comprehensive, and to some, complex looseleaf services is the BNA Labor Relations Reporter. Using the full set of this looseleaf, answer the following:

1. At what page and paragraph does the text of North Dakota labor laws begin?

2. What case is reported at 71 Labor Arbitration Reports 989?

3. What is the address of the Idaho Commission on Human Rights? (Hint -- it serves as the state's fair employment practice agency).

4. What case appears at 18 Fair Employment Practice Cases 966?

5. Where could one find the text of the Export Administration Act?

Drill Problem I:

Using the 1990 CCH Standard Federal Tax Reporter or 1990 Prentice-Hall Federal Taxes 2d as indicated, and the latest edition of A Uniform System of Citation, answer the following and properly cite to the looseleaf.

1. Is a nonresident alien individual who is a member of a partnership which is engaged in business in the U.S. considered to be engaged in business in the U.S.? (CCH)

2. Where can one find commentary on the taxability of prizes and awards? (CCH)

3. Cite a case where a taxpayer's contributions to antiwar groups were not allowed as charitable contributions because a large part of the organization's activities were political. (CCH)

4. Where can one find a discussion of what constitutes "public charities?" (P-H)

5. Where can one find a discussion of the basic rules of collapsible corporations? (P-H)

Chapter 14

Drill Problem II:

Using the 1990 CCH Standard Federal Tax Reporter or 1990 Prentice-Hall Federal Taxes 2d as indicated, answer the following, indicating the paragraph number at which the answer is located.

1. Where can one find Reg. § 1.441-1(a) on the period for computation of taxable income? (CCH)

2. Where is there an explanation of the deduction of expenses for education? (CCH)

3. Under Reg. § 1.403(b) -1(f)(4), how can one determine whether an individual is employed full-time? (P-H)

4. Where is Revenue Ruling 74-298 discussed? (P-H)

CHAPTER 15

SHEPARD'S CITATIONS

ASSIGNMENT 1
USE OF SHEPARD'S UNITED STATES CITATIONS CONSTITUTION

Method:

Refer to Shepard's United States Citations, Statute Edition, United States Constitution. Use bound volumes only. Answer the following questions with reference to the United States Constitution sections listed below. Cite as given in Shepard's.

(1) Give the most recent citation to the official reporter of the Supreme Court of the United States which discussed the section (and clause).

(2) Has the provision been noted in the American Bar Association Journal? If so, cite the most recent reference.

(3) Give the latest A.L.R., A.L.R. Federal or Lawyers' Edition annotation in which the section (and clause) was noted.

Questions:

1. Art. I, §8, cl. 10
2. Art. I, §8, cl. 14
3. Art. I, §8, cl. 18
4. Art. II, §1
5. Art. III, §2, cl. 3
6. Art. IV
7. Art. IV, §1
8. Art. IV, §2
9. Art. V
10. Art. VI
11. Art. VI, cl. 2

Chapter 15

12. Amend. II
13. Amend. III
14. Amend. VII
15. Amend. VIII
16. Amend. IX
17. Amend. X
18. Amend. XII
19. Amend. XIV, §5
20. Amend. XV
21. Amend. XV, §1
22. Amend. XVII
23. Amend XVIII
24. Amend. XXI
25. Amend. XXVI

ASSIGNMENT 2
USE OF SHEPARD'S UNITED STATES CITATIONS - 1982 CODE

Method:

Refer to Shepard's United States Citations, Statute Edition, Code Section. Use bound volumes only. Answer the following questions with reference to the 1982 United States Code sections listed below. Cite as given in Shepard's.

(1) Has the constitutionality of this statute ever been in question? If so, give the holding and the citation(s) of the case(s) so holding. For references to the Supreme Court of the United States, give only the official reporter.

(2) Give the latest A.L.R., A.L.R. Federal or Lawyers' Edition annotation in which the provision was noted.

Questions:

1. Title 1, §109
2. Title 5, §552a, §d, subd. 3
3. Title 7, §1 et seq.
4. Title 8, §1324
5. Title 10, §125
6. Title 12, §1829b
7. Title 15, §15c
8. Title 18, §13
9. Title 18, §956
10. Title 19, §160, §a
11. Title 20, §236 et seq.
12. Title 22, §611, §j
13. Title 23, §131, §e
14. Title 25, §464
15. Title 26, §151 et seq.
16. Title 26, §214
17. Title 28, §1348

Chapter 15

18. Title 29, §201

19. Title 30, §811

20. Title 30, §1275

21. Title 33, §403

22. Title 35, §121

23. Title 40, §270d

24. Title 42, §607

25. Title 47, §315, §a

ASSIGNMENT 3
USE OF STATE SHEPARD'S

Method:

Refer to the Shepard's citator for your state. Use the bound volumes only unless the subject section of the information required can be located only in the temporary supplement to the bound volumes. Cite as given in Shepard's.

Questions:

1. Locate the section in your state citator covering your state's probate code. Select one article or section and answer the following questions:
   (a) Has it been amended, repealed, etc.? If so, answer with the latest citation as given in Shepard's.
   (b) Has it been discussed in a legal periodical? If so, answer with citation as given in Shepard's.
   (c) If available, give the citation to the latest attorney general's opinion citing this article or section.

2. Locate the section in your state citator covering your state's code of criminal procedure. Select one article or section and answer the following questions:
   (a) Give the citation (National Reporter System and official, if available) to the latest case citing this article or section.
   (b) Has it been amended, repealed, etc.? If so, give the latest citation as given in Shepard's.

3. Locate the section in your state citator covering the Uniform Commercial Code. Select one article and section and answer the following questions:
   (a) Has it been amended or repealed by the state legisalature? If so, in what year?
   (b) Give the latest legal periodical citation to this section.

4. Locate the section containing the official reports of the highest court of your state. Select one case from the earliest bound volume of your state's citator. "Shepardize" the case through all subsequent volumes by answering the following questions:
   (a) What is the National Reporter System citation to the same case?
   (b) Give the citation of the case if it is reprinted in another reporter.
   (c) Was the case appealed to the Supreme Court of the United States? If so, what was the result? Give the official citation only.
   (d) Has the holding of the case been criticized, distinguished, overruled, etc., by later decisions? Have these later cases cited the total case or only certain principles? In you answer, designate headnote numbers where necessary.
   (e) Has the opinion been cited by the attorney general of your state? If so, give the latest citation.
   (f) Has the cited opinion been noted in an A.L.R. annotation? If so, give the latest citation.
   (g) Has the case been cited in any legal periodicals? If so, give the citation(s).

5. Locate the section in your state citator containing the National Reporter System regional reporter for your area. Select one case and answer the following questions:
   (a) What is the official citation to the same case?
   (b) Has the case been overruled? If so, cite the overruling case.

6. Locate the section in your state citator containing the Table of Acts by Popular Names or Short Titles. Select one act and answer the following:
   (a) What is citation of the act?
   (b) Are amendments to the act listed in the Table?

7. Locate the section in your state citator covering the rules of the highest court. Select one rule and answer the following questions:
   (a) Has the rule been amended? If so, cite the source where the amendment can be found.
   (b) Has the highest court of your state ever cited this rule? If so, give the citation to the first case citing this rule.
   (c) Has the rule been cited in any legal periodicals? If so, give the citation(s) to the periodical(s).
   (d) Has this rule been cited in any A.L.R. annotation? If so, cite the annotation(s).

8. Locate the section in your state citator covering municipal ordinances or charters.
   (a) From the index to charters determine how many municipalities have been involved in litigation involving public utility rates.
   (b) Select one municipality from the previous question 8(a). Give all citations pertaining to one ordinance or charter provision.

9. Locate the section in your state citator covering the rules of your state bar. Select one rule and answer the following questions:
   (a) Has the constitutionality of this rule ever been questioned? If so, give all citations to that opinion.
   (b) Give the citation (National Reporter System and official, if available) to the latest case citing this rule.
   (c) Has the rule been discussed in legal periodicals? If so, cite one.

ASSIGNMENT 4
USE OF SHEPARD'S UNITED STATES CITATIONS, CASE EDITION

Method:

Refer to Shepard's United States Citations, Case Edition. Use bound volumes of the Case Edition - 1984 only -- do not use any bound supplement volumes. Cite as given in Shepard's. Answer the following questions with reference to the cases listed below.

(1) Give the parallel citation (Lawyers' Edition, Supreme Court Reporter and selected case reporters) for the same case.

(2) Give the citation(s) to the same case in lower courts and/or the United States Supreme Court.

(3) Has this case been cited by the California Supreme Court? If so, give the most recent cite.

(4) Has the case been cited in an American Bar Association Journal article? If so, cite the most recent reference.

Questions:

1. 420 U.S. 283
2. 414 U.S. 395
3. 401 U.S. 82
4. 378 U.S. 478
5. 414 U.S. 168
6. 400 U.S. 309
7. 354 U.S. 449
8. 383 U.S. 541
9. 315 U.S. 501
10. 323 U.S. 471
11. 394 U.S. 721
12. 322 U.S. 292
13. 344 U.S. 183
14. 319 U.S. 182

Chapter 15

15. 367 U.S. 488

16. 400 U.S. 25

17. 346 U.S. 235

18. 391 U.S. 123

19. 346 U.S. 389

20. 339 U.S. 460

ASSIGNMENT 5
USE OF SHEPARD'S FEDERAL CITATIONS, FEDERAL REPORTER

Method:

Refer to Shepard's Federal Citations, Federal Reporter. Use bound volumes only. Answer the following with reference to the cases listed below. Each citation is followed by a Topic and Key Number form the Federal Reporter syllabus to the cited case. This identifies a specific numbered headnote in the cited case. Examine the cited case in the Federal Reporter, and identify the headnote number.

(1) Give the federal cases which distinguished this specific point of law of the cited case by subsequent decisions. Give only Federal Reporter and Federal Supplement citations. Cite as given in Shepard's but omit the superior numbers in your answers.

(2) List the opinions which relate to the specific headnote but have no analytical symbol preceding the citation. Give only the most recent Federal Reporter and/or Federal Supplement citations. Cite as given in Shepard's but omit the superior numbers in your answers.

Questions:

1.	458 F.2d 1323.	Courts - Key #284
2.	398 F.2d 722.	Labor Relations - Key #574
3.	413 F.2d 459.	Criminal Law - Key #517.1(1)
4.	456 F.2d 112.	Civil Rights - Key #43, 44(1)
5.	453 F.2d 54.	Schools and school districts - Key #172
6.	442 F.2d 698.	Criminal Law - Key #304(1)
7.	430 F.2d 771.	Constitutional Law - Key #272, Prisons - Key #13
8.	453 F.2d 661.	Criminal Law - Key #1213
9.	450 F.2d 199.	Grand Jury - Key #36
10.	371 F.2d 911.	Habeas Corpus - Key #59
11.	295 F.2d 531.	Criminal Law - Key #823(5)
12.	330 F.2d 859.	Federal Civil Procedure - Key #1960

13.	333 F.2d 535.	Criminal Law - Key #275, 1026
14.	105 F.2d 331.	Monopolies - Key #28(6)
15.	171 F. 305.	Corporations - Key #560

ASSIGNMENT 6
USE OF SHEPARD'S FEDERAL CITATIONS - FEDERAL SUPPLEMENT, FEDERAL RULES DECISIONS, COURT OF CLAIMS

Method:

Refer to Shepard's Federal Citations: Federal Supplement, Federal Rules Decisions, Court of Claims. Use bound volumes only. Answer the following questions with reference to the cases listed below. Cite as given in Shepard's.

(1) Was the cited case appealed to a United States Court of Appeals? If the action of the court is indicated (e.g., affirmed, dismissed, modified, reversed) specify the action and give the latest citation to the National Reporter System.

(2) Was the cited case appealed to the Supreme Court of the United States? If the action of the Court is indicated (e.g., affirmed, dismissed, modified, reversed) specify the action and give the latest citatiion to the official reporter.

(3) Give the latest A.L.R., A.L.R. Federal or Lawyers' Edition annotation in which the cited case was noted. Disregard superior numbers.

Questions:

1. 3 F. Supp. 909
2. 29 F. Supp. 436
3. 38 Ct. Cl. 10
4. 30 F. Supp. 570
5. 30 F.R.D. 3
6. 235 F. Supp. 183
7. 59 Ct. Cl. 593
8. 2 F.R.D. 270
9. 192 F. Supp. 170
10. 87 F. Supp. 691
11. 136 Ct. Cl. 324
12. 200 F. Supp. 653

13. 99 Ct. Cl. 1

14. 37 F.R.D. 330

15. 236 F. Supp. 56

16. 21 F.R.D. 335

17. 342 F. Supp. 616

18. 191 Ct. Cl. 191

19. 43 F.R.D. 308

20. 21 F.R.D. 335

ASSIGNMENT 7
USE OF SHEPARD'S UNITED STATES - STATUTES AT LARGE

Method:

Refer to Shepard's United States Citations, Statute Edition, United States Statutes at Large, 1986 (not included in the United States Code) Section. Use bound volumes only. Answer the following questions with reference to the sections of the Statutes at Large which are not included in the United States Code listed below. Cite as given in Shepard's.

(1) Cite any act of Congress noted as affecting this statute and briefly give the effect (e.g., amended, repealed, etc.) of such act.

(2) Give the latest citing of the statute by the Supreme Court of the United States. Give the official reporter citation only.

Questions:

1. 1789, July 4, ch. 2, §1, 1 Stat. 24
2. 1809, March 1, ch. 24, 2 Stat. 528
3. 1870, May 31, ch. 114, §4, 16 Stat. 140
4. 1875, Feb. 8, ch. 36, §18, 18 Stat. 307
5. 1902, May 27, ch. 888, 32 Stat. 245
6. 1921, May 19, ch. 8, 42 Stat. 5
7. 1927, Jan. 21, ch. 47, §1, 44 Stat. 1010
8. 1935, Aug. 30, ch. 829, §105, 49 Stat. 1014
9. 1940, July 2, ch. 508, §1, 54 Stat. 712
10. 1948, April 3, ch. 169, §101, 62 Stat. 137
11. 1958, July 7, P.L. 85-508, §4, 72 Stat. 339
12. 1789, July 4, ch. 2, 1 Stat. 24
13. 1801, Feb. 27, ch. 15, 2 Stat. 103
14. 1836, April 20, ch. 54, 5 Stat. 10
15. 1889, Jan. 14, ch. 24, 25 Stat. 642

16. 1901, March 3, ch. 854, §823, 31 Stat. 1189
17. 1906, June 20, ch. 3446, §2, 34 Stat. 316
18. 1959, Sept. 14, P.L. 86-272, §201, 73 Stat. 555
19. 1897, June 7, ch. 3, §1, 30 Stat. 62
20. 1919, Oct. 28, ch. 85, 41 Stat. 305

ASSIGNMENT 8
USE OF SHEPARD'S REGIONAL REPORTER CITATIONS

Method:

Refer to Shepard's Regional Reporter Citations. Use bound volumes only. Answer the following questions with reference to the cases listed below. Cite as given in Shepard's.

(1) Give the official citation of the case.

(2) Has the cited case been appealed to the Supreme Court of the United States? If appealed, give the official reporter citation.

(3) Do any of Shepard's symbols indicate that the cited case has been criticized, followed, overruled, etc., by subsequent decisions? If so indicated, designate the headnote number of the citing case. Disregard dissenting opinions.

(4) List all other states and the District of Columbia which have cited this opinion.

Questions:

1. 201 A.2d 715
2. 182 A.2d 596
3. 66 N.E.2d 888
4. 95 N.W.2d 273
5. 10 P.2d 597
6. 61 P.2d 293
7. 106 P.2d 755
8. 237 S.W. 786
9. 244 S.W. 549
10. 78 S.E.2d 462
11. 86 S.E.2d 114
12. 155 So.2d 586
13. 252 A.2d 580

14. 198 N.E.2d 590
15. 34 N.W. 1
16. 69 P. 564
17. 393 S.W.2d 739
18. 260 A.2d 68
19. 241 A.2d 691
20. 221 N.E.2d 543
21. 183 N.E.2d 579
22. 78 N.W.2d 509
23. 192 N.W.2d 466
24. 450 P.2d 775
25. 416 P.2d 67
26. 124 S.E. 2d 653
27. 108 S.E.2d 328
28. 243 S.W.2d 683
29. 523 S.W.2d 377
30. 93 So.2d 769

ASSIGNMENT 9
USE OF SHEPARD'S ACTS AND CASES BY POPULAR NAMES

Method:

Refer to Shepard's Acts and Cases by Popular Names. Use 1986 bound volume. Answer the following questions. Cite as given in Shepard's.

Questions:

1. (a) Give the citation for the Golden Nematode Act.
   (b) When was it enacted?

2. How many states have enacted Sunshine Laws?

3. What is the U.S. Supreme Court citation for the Busing case?

4. Give the citation to the Watergate Tapes Case.

5. Where can the Fugitive Slave Law case be found?

6. Give citations to the Aircraft Hi-Jacking Act.

7. Give citations to the Negligent Attorney case.

8. Cite Oklahoma's Law Library Act.

9. What government administrative agency ruled on the Station Facilities case? Cite the agency report of the case.

10. Give the citations to the latest U.S. Supreme Court reports on the Girard College Cases.

11. How many states have No-Knock Acts? Give citations to these acts.

12. Give the citation to the Colorado Narcotic Drug Act.

13. (a) Give the citation for the Citizens Abroad Act.
    (b) When was it enacted?

14. Give the citation to the Theatrical Productions Case.

15. How many states have adopted a Sick Leave Act?

16. Give the citation to the earliest enactment of the Removal of Causes Acts.

17. Give the citation to the Municipal Railway Election case.

18. How many "Mutt and Jeff" cases have been reported?

19. Give the citations to the Milk, Cream and Butterfat case.

20. Give the citations to the Moldy Tomato Paste case.

21. Give the citation to the latest Mutual Security Act.

22. Give the citation to the New Jersey Narcotic and Drug Abuse Control Act.

23. Has Nebraska enacted an Air-Raid Precautions Act?

24. Give the citation to the official report of the U.S. Supreme Court in the Federal Maternity Act case.

25. Give the citation to the Fowler Hotel case.

26. Give the citations to the Bob-Tail case.

27. How many Group Discrimination cases have been reported?

28. Give the citations to the Cutler case.

29. Give the citations to the Rat case.

30. (a) Was the Betty Boop case heard before the U.S. Supreme Court?
    (b) Give the citation to the first reported opinion in the Betty Boop case.

31. Give the citation to the Mystic River Dam Loan Act.

32. Give the citation for the Electric Companies Act.

33. Give the latest citation to the Forty-Three Gallons of Cognac Brandy case.

34. How many states have adopted a Commercial Feed Act?

35. Does New Hampshire have an Elevator Act?

ASSIGNMENT 10
THEME AND DRILL PROBLEMS

Theme Problem I:

Find the place that the Brown decision (347 U.S. 483) first appears in Shepard's United States Citations--Cases Edition and, using that volume, answer the following questions:

1. Give the parallel citations.
2. What Missouri cases cite Brown?
3. Where in 373 U.S. is Brown cited in dissent?
4. What Alabama cases cite Brown?
5. Where was Brown cited in 401 U.S.?
6. Where in volume 59 of the A.B.A. Journal will the case be mentioned?
7. Has it been overruled?
8. What Florida case in 342 So.2d cites it?
9. Where in 433 U.S. is it followed?
10. Where is it cited in 64 A.B.A. Journal?

Theme Problem II:

Locate the first appearance of Roe v. Wade, 410 U.S. 113, in Shepard's United States Citations--Case Edition and, using that volume, answer the following questions;

1. Give the parallel citations.
2. Where is the denial of a rehearing reported?
3. What South Dakota case cites it?
4. What Federal District Court opinions "harmonize" it?
5. Has it been overruled?
6. Where in 63 A.B.A. Journal is it cited?
7. Where in 431 U.S. is it distinguished?

Chapter 15

Theme Problem III:

Find the first appearance of Gideon v. Wainwright, 372 U.S. 335, in Shepard's United States Citations--Case Edition and, using that volume, answer the following questions:

1. Give the parallel citations.
2. What is the first time it is cited in dissent?
3. What is the first Idaho decision listed?
4. What is the first A.B.A. Journal citation listed?
5. Has it been overruled or reversed?
6. Where is the first time the decision is "explained"?
7. What is the first Arkansas decision cited?
8. Where in volume 58 of the A.B.A. Journal is it mentioned?
9. Where is it cited in 433 U.S.?
10. Where is it cited in 265 N.W.2d?

Drill Problem I:

A. Using only bound volumes of Shepard's United States Citations--Case Edition, answer the following questions for each of the citations listed below:

(1) What is the first case listed that cited the decision in dissent?

(2) List the first citation (if there are any) to the A.B.A. Journal.

(3) Give the parallel citations.

(4) Has the case been reversed or overruled?

1. 397 U.S. 254
2. 406 U.S. 441
3. 93 S.Ct. 2405

B. Using only bound volumes of Shepard's Federal Citations--Cases, answer the following questions for each citation listed below:

(1) List the first case cited from the 1st circuit, if any.

(2) List the first case listed that followed the decision.

(3) Has it been reversed or overruled?

(4) If there is an A.L.R. citation, list it.

1. 469 F.2d 1377

2. 496 F.2d 1303

3. 220 F. 545

C. Using only bound volumes of the regional Shepard's, answer the following questions for each citation listed below:

(1) List the first case that cites the decision in dissent.

(2) Cite the first regional reporter case listed.

(3) Give the parallel citation.

(4) Has the decision been reversed?

1. 71 P. 453

2. 208 S.E.2d 459

3. 131 N.W.2d 293

D. Using the 1986 bound volumes of Shepard's United States Citations--Statute Edition, answer the following questions for each citation listed below:

(1) Give the first U.S. Supreme Court citation listed, if any.

(2) Has its constitutionality been adjudicated? If yes, list the first citation.

(3) Give the first A.L.R. Federal citation listed.

1. 42 U.S.C. §3613

2. 10 U.S.C. §1552

3. 12 U.S.C. §1762

E. Using the 1986 bound volume of Shepard's United States Citations--Statute Edition--U.S. Constitution, answer the following questions for each citation listed below:

(1) Give the first citation to a U.S. Supreme Court case, if any.

(2) Give first citation to A.L.R., if any.

(3) Any special action (i.e., amended) noted? If so, provide first citation.

1. Art. III, §1

2. Art. II, §1

Drill Problem II:

A. Using only bound volumes of Shepard's United States Citations-Case Edition, answer the following questions for each citation listed below:

(1) What is the first case listed that cited the decision in dissent?

(2) List the first citation to the A.B.A. Journal, if any.

(3) Give the parallel citations.

(4) Has the case been reversed or overruled?

1. 360 U.S. 264

2. 403 U.S. 388

3. 36 L.E.2d 366

B. Using only bound volumes of Shepard's Federal Citations--Cases, answer the following questions for each citation listed below:

(1) List the first case cited from the 1st Circuit.

(2) List the first case listed that followed the decision.

(3) Has it been reversed or overruled?

(4) If there is an A.L.R. cite, list it.

1. 415 F.2d 1185

2. 505 F.2d 977

3. 67 F.2d 585

4. 323 F. Supp. 799

C. Using only bound volumes of the regional Shepard's, answer the following questions for each citation listed below:

(1) List the first case that cites the decision in dissent.

(2) Cite the first regional reporter case listed.

(3) Give the parallel citation.

(4) Has the decision been reversed?

1. 34 P.2d 534

2. 1 So. 273

3. 256 N.E.2d 384

D. Using the 1986 bound volumes of Shepard's United States Citations--Statute Edition--U.S. Code 1982, answer the following questions for each citation listed below:

(1) Give the first U.S. Supreme Court citation listed, if any.

(2) Has its constitutionality been adjudged? If yes, list the first citation.

(3) Give the First A.L.R. Fed. citation listed.

1. 33 U.S.C. 407

2. 45 U.S.C. 153(1)(p)

E. Using the 1986 bound volumes of Shepard's United States Citations--Statute Edition--U.S. Constitution, answer the following questions for each citation listed below:

(1) Give the first citation to a U.S. Supreme Court case, if any.

(2) Give first citation to A.L.R., if any.

(3) Any special action (i.e., amended) noted? If so, provide first citation.

1. Amendment IX

2. Amendment XVIII

Drill Problem III:

A. Using only bound volumes of Shepard's United States Citations--Case Edition, answer the following questions for each citation listed below:

(1) What is the first case listed that cited the decision in dissent?

(2) List the first citation to the A.B.A. Journal, if any.

(3) Give the parallel citations.

(4) Has the case been reversed or overruled?

1. 346 U.S. 1

2. 397 U.S. 471

3. 256 U.S. 135

B. Using only bound volumes of Shepard's Federal Citations, answer the following questions for each citation listed below:

(1) List the first case cited from the 1st Circuit.

(2) List the first case listed that followed the decision.

(3) Has it been reversed or overruled?

(4) If there is an A.L.R. citation, list it.

1. 471 F.2d 488

2. 185 F.2d 622

3. 62 F. Supp. 73

4. 340 F. Supp. 1343

C. Using the appropriate bound volume of regional Shepard's --Cases, answer the following questions for each citation listed below:

(1) List the first case that cites the decision in dissent.

(2) Cite the first regional reporter case listed.

(3) Give the parallel citation.

(4) Has the decision been reversed?

1. 236 S.W.2d 772

2. 337 A.2d 893

3. 181 N.W.2d 811

D. Using the 1986 bound volumes to Shepard's United States Citations--Statute Edition, answer the following questions for each citation listed below:

(1) Give the first U.S. Supreme Court citation listed, if any.

(2) Has its constitutionality been adjudged? If yes, list the first citation.

(3) Give the first A.L.R. Fed. citatiion listed.

1. 18 U.S.C. §2520

2. 28 U.S.C. §2111

3. 82 Stat. 815 §23

E. Using the 1986 bound volumes of Shepard's United States Citations--Statute Edition--U.S. Constitution, answer the following questions for each citation listed below:

(1) Give the first citation to a U.S. Supreme Court case, if any.

(2) Give first citation to A.L.R., if any.

(3) Any special action (i.e., amended) noted? If so, provide first citation.

1. Art. 1, §6, cl.1

2. Amendment 1

CHAPTER 16

LEGAL ENCYCLOPEDIAS

ASSIGNMENT 1
THE INDEX METHOD WITH AMERICAN JURISPRUDENCE 2D AND CORPUS JURIS SECUNDUM

Method:

Analyze each of the following problems for words, expressed or implied, which should be in the general index or specific volume index of the encyclopedia abbreviated in the parenthesis following each problem. A completed answer to each problem should contain the following parts:

(1) A tentative answer to the legal problems;

(2) Word(s) in the index under which the encyclopedic text was found;

(3) Identification of index in which word was found (i.e., "volume index" or "general index");

(4) Citation to the encyclopedic text in which the tentative answer was discovered.

This citation should be expressed in the form set out in the latest edition of A Uniform System of Citation.

Example:

QUESTION: Are advertising signs, with useful lives of more than one year, subject to depreciation under federal taxation laws? (Am. Jur. 2d)

ANSWER:
(1) Yes
(2) Depreciation -- advertising signs
(3) Volume index
(4) 34 Am. Jur. 2d Federal Taxation §5565 (1990).

Questions:

1. In a civil proceeding aimed at removal of environmental pollution is a preponderance of the evidence sufficient to establish violation of statute? (C.J.S.).

2. Was the Korean conflict a war in the constitutional or legal sense? (Am. Jur. 2d).

3. Did the Nineteenth Amendment confer upon women the right to vote? (C.J.S.).

4. Is it possible for a law student to find the latest compilation of "Minimum Requirements for Admission to Legal Practice in the United States" in <u>American Jurisprudence 2d</u>? (Desk Book).

5. According to recent authority, in a juvenile court proceeding, are juveniles entitled to constitutional protection against twice being placed in jeopardy for the same offense? (Am. Jur. 2d).

6. Can a court take judicial notice that a sonic boom caused by a jet aircraft flying at low altitude was an explosion? (C.J.S.).

7. Is a professional baseball league a "business operated for gain or profit," within the meaning of the Workmen's Compensation Act? (Am. Jur. 2d).

8. Does a person who enters the military service lose thereby the domicile which he had before he entered the service? (Am. Jur. 2d).

9. In a trial, must the plaintiff ordinarily establish his prima facie case before cross-examination of defendant's witnesses? (C.J.S.).

10. Is a student at a state college entitled to notice and hearing before being expelled for misconduct? (Am. Jur. 2d).

11. In the absence of a statute, is a conversation between an accountant and his client a privileged communication? (Am. Jur. 2d).

12. May a person, who has a right to treat an absolute deed as a mortgage, lose the right through laches, or prejudicial delay? (C.J.S.).

13. If a woman agrees to care for and nurse a man for the rest of his life in return for his promise to will her all his property, will their agreement be invalidated by their future illicit cohabitation? (C.J.S.).

14. Are punchboards exempted from the federal wagering taxes? (Am. Jur. 2d).

15. Is competition an essential element of the offense of "drag racing?" (C.J.S.).

16. Can the "Equal Rights for Men and Women" proposed Constitutional Amendment be located in <u>American Jurisprudence 2d</u>? (Desk Book).

17. Does a parent's failure to support his child by itself constitute such abandonment, desertion or neglect which would permit adoption without the parent's consent? (C.J.S.).

18. In order to challenge a juror for cause based upon bias or prejudice may the juror be examined concerning his relationships with parties to the action, counsel, prospective witnesses, or other persons interested in the action who are not parties of record? (C.J.S.).

19. May a court disbar an attorney for defamatory criticisms of judicial acts incorporated in a brief? (Am. Jur. 2d).

20. Is a district or prosecuting attorney of a state entitled to extra compensation when he has a duty to perform services in another county in connection with a suit to which his county is a party? (C.J.S.).

21. May the family purpose doctrine be applied to impose tort liability for personal injury on a family corporation which owns the automobile in question and maintains it for general family use? (C.J.S.).

22. Will a tenant at sufferance be liable to his landlord for an injury to the premises which was caused by a fire resulting from the tenant's negligence? (C.J.S.).

23. Does public policy require that a state recognize a bilateral Mexican divorce as a matter of comity? (Am. Jur. 2d).

24. Must other vessels exercise care to avoid a collision with a vessel which has obstructed a narrow channel? (C.J.S.).

25. Is an infant liable on the basis of quasi-contract for the value of necessaries furnished him? (Am. Jur. 2d).

26. Is a state barred from making payment of a poll tax a prerequisite to voting? (Am Jur. 2d).

27. Is the concealment in a licensing proceeding of a prior arrest record a ground for the refusal of an application for a license to sell intoxicating liquors? (Am. Jur. 2d).

28. Will an inexperienced student pilot be held to have assumed the risk of downdraft which causes the crash of an airplane if he has had no training in meteorology? (C.J.S.).

29. May a material false statement made under oath in connection with an application for a marriage license constitute perjury? (Am. Jur. 2d).

30. Are federal war risk insurance statutes affecting seamen intended to provide insurance protection to dependents in case of loss of life or bodily injury to seamen? (C.J.S.).

31. Is the Postal Service authorized to prescribe regulations for the exclusion or withdrawal of nonmailable matter from the mail? (Am. Jur. 2d).

32. If a factor has made advances on consigned goods, is he bound to accept and pay a draft drawn on him by the principal before the advances are repaid? (C.J.S.)

33. Does the federal crime of seditious conspiracy require an overt act for its completion? (Am. Jur. 2d).

34. Is the manufacture of meat products from horsemeat illegal as a violation of a regulation prohibiting the manufacture for sale of adulterated food if there is no attempt to conceal the fact the product is horsement? (C.J.S.).

35. Does a builder have an obligation to perform extra work without compensation if that work is not specified in the construction plans which themselves form a part of the contract? (C.J.S.).

36. If an attached garage is not so attached to the house as to present the appearance of being an integral part of the dwelling house, is it an accessory building within the meaning of zoning ordinances which restrict the location of accessory buildings to the rear half of the lot? (Am. Jur. 2d).

37. Have courts found that the freedom of religion of Jewish persons is violated by Sunday closing laws? (Am. Jur. 2d).

38. Under the Lanham Act, will the type of product for which a trademark is to be registered affect whether or not the mark is considered scandalous? (C.J.S.).

39. Do the statutes regulating telephone companies include within their scope the operation of a two-way mobile radio system? (Am. Jur. 2d).

40. Can a material misrepresentation be implied from the exhibiting of fraudulent or misleading maps or plats? (Am. Jur. 2d).

ASSIGNMENT 2
USE OF THE TOPIC METHOD WITH AMERICAN JURISPRUDENCE 2D AND CORPUS JURIS SECUNDUM

Method:

Analyze each of the problems below for words, expressed or implied, to determine the suggested topic(s). Using the encyclopedia indicated in the parenthesis following each problem, turn to the topic's "analysis" or list of major subject divisions and then to the more detailed "sub-analysis" or section outline. Your answer whould contain the following information:

(1) Answer to the legal problem posed.

(2) A citation to the encyclopedic text in which the answer was found.

Follow the citation form set out in the latest edition of A Uniform System of Citation.

Example:

QUESTION: May an offer of a reward be revoked at any time before it is accepted by performance?
ANSWER: (1) Yes
(2) 67 Am. Jur. 2d Rewards §15 (1985).

Questions:

1. Do ordinary officers and agents of a corporation have the power to borrow money on behalf of the corporation? (C.J.S.).

2. Is probable cause necessary in order for customs officers to conduct a search of vehicles allegedly bringing narcotics or dangerous drugs into the United States? (C.J.S.).

3. May a railroad company acquire title to land by adverse possession or prescription? (C.J.S.).

4. Does the assignment of the interest of a vendor or vendee in a contract for the sale of land as security for a debt create an equitable mortgage? (C.J.S.).

5. Is the Securities and Exchange Commission authorized to subpoena witnesses and to require the production of relevant books, papers and documents? (C.J.S.).

6. Does mere inaction constitute negligence where a duty has been undertaken gratuitously? (C.J.S.).

7. Can a municipal corporation be held civilly liable for its failure to enact or enforce ordinances? (C.J.S.).

8. May the crime of forgery be committed by the signing of a fictitious or assumed name? (Am. Jur. 2d).

9. Are unavoidably unsafe products classified as unreasonably dangerous for purposes of the strict liability doctrine when they are accompanied by proper directions and warnings? (Am. Jur. 2d).

10. May a state ever take or authorize the taking of property situated in another state under its powers of eminent domain? (Am. Jur. 2d).

11. Must an overt act be of a criminal nature in order to warrant conviction for treason? (Am. Jur. 2d).

12. May a false statement on an income tax return constitute perjury? (Am. Jur. 2d).

13. Is the offense of fraudulent enlistment in the military service exclusively a military offense punishable only by court-martial? (Am. Jur. 2d).

14. May a corporation legally change or alter the name originally selected by it without recourse to formal proceedings? (Am. Jur. 2d).

15. Can a change in the law render a contract illegal which was legal when made? (C.J.S.).

16. In order to secure relief on the ground of fraud, must the complainant have a right to rely upon the misrepresentation? (Am. Jur. 2d).

17. Does the law impose on the bailee the duty of insuring the subject matter of the bailment? (C.J.S.).

18. Will refusal to permit challenges and watchers to be present at the polls, during the conduct of an election, invalidate the election? (C.J.S.).

19. May the release of mutual claims by each of two persons constitute an accord and satisfaction? (C.J.S.).

20. In order to constitute an escrow must the deposit be irrevocable? (Am. Jur. 2d).

21. May a failure, with excuse, to obey a court order to pay money, constitute contempt? (C.J.S.).

22. Is a wife obliged to furnish her husband with a home, if she had one and he does not have a home? (Am. Jur. 2d).

23. May a will be revoked by oral declaration? (C.J.S.).

24. Does a state Sunday closing law violate the U.S. Constitution respecting establishment of religion, where the present purpose and effect of the statute is not to aid religion, but to set aside a day of rest and recreation? (Am. Jur. 2d).

25. May franchises be condemned under the right of eminent domain? (C.J.S.).

26. Is a state statute prohibiting desertion and nonsupport of unborn children valid? (Am. Jur. 2d).

27. Is a contract for the sale of standing timber within the Statute of Frauds? (C.J.S.).

28. May a qualified expert testify from the nature of a wound as to the character of the weapon which inflicted or could have inflicted the wound? (Am. Jur. 2d).

29. Is the state regarded as a party to every divorce proceeding? (C.J.S.).

30. Will the court grant a decree of specific performance of a binding oral contract? (Am. Jur. 2d).

31. Under the Bankruptcy Act, may receivers or trustees be held liable personally or on their bonds to the United States for penalties or forfeitures incurred by the bankrupts? (Am. Jur. 2d).

32. Will jurisdiction for a declaratory judgment be entertained where another equally appropriate remedy is already available? (C.J.S.).

33. May a person maintain a proceeding for a variance from a zoning law, if his sole purpose is to obtain a higher valuation in condemnation proceedings? (C.J.S.).

34. Is an employer prohibited by law from executing a "yellow dog contract," in which the employee agrees that he will not become a member of a labor union? (Am. Jur. 2d).

35. May a beneficiary under a trust deed foreclose a mortgage on the trust property, when the trustee neglects to do so? (C.J.S.)

ASSIGNMENT 3
DRILL PROBLEMS FOR LEGAL ENCYCLOPEDIAS

Instructions:

For each of the following questions:

(1) provide a "yes" or "no" answer;

(2) cite the volume, title and section of the encyclopedia under which the correct answer can be found.

The answer should be in proper citation form according to the latest edition of A Uniform System of Citation.

Drill Problem I:

A. Use C.J.S. to answer the following questions:

1. Are children born of parents who are subject to jurisdiction of a country considered citizens of that country even if their parents are aliens?

2. Does the fact of a brother-sister relationship imply that there should be a presumption that service rendered or work performed is gratuitous?

3. Does simple pursuit of game confer on a hunter a right of ownership?

B. Use Am. Jur. 2d to answer the following questions:

1. (Use Title Index to Descent and Distribution). When a person is sentenced to life imprisonment, can his/her property then be distributed as if death had occurred?

2. Is an owner who burns his/her house while it is in the possession of another guilty of arson?

Drill Problem II:

A. Use C.J.S. to answer the following questions:

1. Is a statement as to genealogy admissible as an exception to the heresay rule?

2. Was the utterance of obscene words in public indictable at common law?

B. Use Am. Jur. 2d to answer the following questions:

1. Have the Courts traditionally viewed the use of threats or force to recover gambling losses as "robbery?"

2. If unruly spectators may have caused prejudice in a trial, can the verdict be appealed?

3. Can one find discussion and text of Federal Rules of Evidence? Where?

<u>Drill Problem III</u>:

A. Use C.J.S. to answer the following questions:

1. Under negligence theory, if someone habitually trespasses upon your land, does your knowledge of the trespass create a duty of care for the trespasser's safety?

2. Can counsel use medical texts on the cross examination of an expert witness?

B. Use Am. Jur. 2d to answer the following questions:

1. Does the act of advertising to treat patients by mail by means of "mental science" show a scheme to use the mails of the United States Post Office for fraud absent any other proof?

2. Does one need corroboration of the testimony of one of the parties to probe the crime of adultery?

CHAPTER 17

LEGAL PERIODICALS AND INDEXES

ASSIGNMENT 1
AUTHOR INDEX PROBLEMS -- INDEX TO LEGAL PERIODICALS, CURRENT LAW INDEX, LEGAL RESOURCE INDEX, LEGALTRAC

PART I.

Method: Using the Index to Legal Periodicals, locate and cite the following:

Questions:

	Date	Author	Subject
1.	1973	R. H. Freilich	Missouri law of land use controls
2.	1969	R. A. Jensen	Effect of federal truth in lending act
3.	1957	L. R. Powell, Jr.	Contributory negligence
4.	1970	J. O. Newman	Prosecutor and defender reform
5.	1975	R. B. Ginsburg	Gender and the Constitution
6.	1967	P. J. Rohan	Perfecting the condominium as a housing tool
7.	1942	W. H. Pedrick	War measures and contract liability
8.	1961	W. H. Rehnquist	Subdivision trusts and the bankruptcy act
9.	1959	I. Younger	Congressional investigations and executive secrecy
10.	1973	J. T. Sneed	Charitable remainder trusts
11.	1962	K. N. Llewellyn	Lecture on appellate advocacy
12.	1961	S. Mentschikoff	Commercial arbitration
13.	1948	J. B. Fordham	Home rule powers in theory and practice
14.	1970	J. O'Connell	Public opinion on no-fault auto insurance

15.	1969	H. Couch	Realistic divorce law
16.	1971	S. T. Agnew	Case for revenue sharing
17.	1971	R. M. Nixon	To improve the process of justice
18.	1972	T. F. Eagleton	Congress and the war powers
19.	1971	R. E. Keeton	No-fault insurance: a status report
20.	1964	R. F. Kennedy	Halfway houses pay off

PART II. Using Current Law Index, locate and cite the following:

Questions:

	Date	Author	Subject
1.	1981	Paul Verkuil	Judicial review of informal rulemaking
2.	1981	Aviam Soifer	Complacency and constitutional law
3.	1980	Albert Borowitz	Harvard murder case
4.	1982	William Epstein	Dialectics and American legal education
5.	1983	Robert Gorman	Recording musician and union power
6.	1984	Sylvia Law	Sex and the Constitution
7.	1984	Gerald Frug	Ideology of bureaucracy in American law
8.	1984	Monroe Price	Text and intellect
9.	1984	Leonard Levy	Origins of free press clause
10.	1985	Abner Mikva	Footnotes

PART III. Using Legal Resource Index, locate and cite the following:

Questions:

	Date	Author	Subject
1.	1981	Peter M. Gerhardt	Competitive advantages explanation for intrabrand restraints

2.	1984	Robert J. Levy	Pearson-Thoennes study and mediation
3.	1982	James Brook	Contractual disclaimer and limitation of liability under the law of New York
4.	1981	Janice E. Kosel	The discharge of student loans in bankruptcy
5.	1986	Paul J. Mastrangelo	A mediography on the Supreme Court.
6.	1985	Lee Modjeska	The Reagan NLRB
7.	1985	Blanka Kudej	International Monetary Fund bibliography
8.	1985	Edward Re	Legal writing as good literature
9.	1983	Antonin Scalia	Standing as an essential element of the separation of powers
10.	1980	Kathleen M. Carrick	A case study approach to legal research

PART IV. Using LegalTrac, locate and cite the following:

Questions:

	Date	Author	Subject
1.	1985	Ralph S. Brown	Eligibility for copyright protection
2.	1986	Robert Bennett	Judges and original intent
3.	1983	Roberto Ungar	The Critical Legal Studies movement
4.	1984	Gerald Korngold	Privately held conservation servitudes
5.	1984	Michael Tigar	Mail fraud
6.	1981	Lawrence Tribe	Jurisdictional gerrymandering
7.	1985	Fred R. Shapiro	Most-cited law review articles
8.	1984	Francis X. Beytaugh	Privacy in perspective
9.	1983	John Hart Ely	Business law vs. public interest law
10.	1985	Mark G. Yudof	Effective schools and federal and state constitutions

ASSIGNMENT 2
CASE APPROACH TO PERIODICAL ARTICLES

PART I.

Method:

Using the Index to Legal Periodicals, locate and cite the first (by date of law review issue) student comment on the following cases:

	Year of Comment	Case
1.	1968	In Re Permian Basin Area Rate Cases, 88 S.Ct. 1344 (1968).
2.	1972	People v. McKinnon, 7 Cal.3d 889, 500 P.2d 1097 (1972).
3.	1973	Nathan Cummings, 61 T.C. 1 (1973).
4.	1966	Office of Communication of the United Church of Christ v. FCC, 359 F.2d 994 (D.C. Cir. 1966).
5.	1971	Investors Management Co., SEC Exchange Act Release No. 9267, CCH Fed.Sec. L.Rep. para. 78,163 (1971).
6.	1968	Hopkins v. Gardner, 374 F.2d 726.
7.	1972	U.S. v. 16179 Molso Italian .22 Caliber Winlee Derringer Convertible Starter Guns, 433 F.2d 463.
8.	1973	Brasserie de Haecht v. Wilkin-Janssen Case 43 Paragraph 72 (1973) C.M.L.R. 287.
9.	1968	Hicks v. Hicks, 155 S.E.2d 799.
10.	1971	Davis v. Thornton, 180 N.W.2d 11.
11.	1972	DeFunis v. Odegaard, No. 741727 (Washington Superior Court for King County, Sept. 22, 1971).
12.	1957	Federal Trade Commission v. B. F. Goodrich Co., 242 F.2d 31.
13.	1966	Lorenz v. State, 406 P.2d 278.
14.	1962	Communist Party of the U.S. v. Catherwood, 81 S.Ct. 1465.
15.	1949	Hialeah Race Course, Inc. v. Gulfstream Park Racing Association, Inc., 37 So.2d 692.

16.	1959	Tuscarora Indian Nation v. FPC, 265 F.2d 338.
17.	1967	Hoffa v. U.S., 87 S.Ct. 408.
18.	1949	Alden-Rochelle, Inc. v. American Society of Composers, Authors and Publishers, 80 F. Supp. 888.
19.	1938	City of Mangum v. Brownlee, 75 P.2d 174.
20.	1967	Award of Her Majesty Queen Elizabeth II for the Arbitration of a Controversy Between the Argentine Republic and the Republic of Chile Concerning Certain Parts of the Boundary Between Their Territories, Court of Arbitration November 24, 1966.

PART II. Using Current Law Index, locate and give the citation for a periodical article for each of the following cases:

	Year	Case
1.	1980	The Despina R, (1979) 1 Lloyds Rep. 1 (H.L.).
2.	1981	State ex rel. McCamic v. McCoy, 276 S.E.2d 534 (1981).
3.	1982	City of Berkeley v. Superior Court, 606 P.2d 362 (1980).
4.	1982	St. Martin Evangelical Lutheran Church v. South Dakota, 101 S. Ct. 2142 (1981).
5.	1983	In re Doe, 440 A.2d 712 (1982).
6.	1983	People v. Bustamante, 634 P.2d 927 (1981).
7.	1984	MBL (USA) Corp. v. Diekman, 445 N.E.2d 418 (1983).
8.	1984	In re Estate of Bartlett, 680 P.2d 369 (1984).
9.	1985	Watt v. California, 104 S. Ct. 656 (1984).
10.	1985	Colombia v. Peru, 1950 I.C.J. 266.

Chapter 17

PART III. Using Legal Resource Index, locate and give the citation for a periodical article for each of the following cases:

Questions:

	Year	Case
1.	1986	City of Auburn v. Mavis, 468 N.E.2d 548 (1984).
2.	1980	First National City Bank v. Banco Nacional de Cuba, 431 F.2d 394 (1970).
3.	1986	Harvey C. Smith Drugs Ltd. v. MNR, 1 C.T.C. 2339 (1986).
4.	1985	In re Highfield Commodities Ltd., (1984) 3 All E.R. 884 (ch.).
5.	1986	Union, Local 11 v. NLRB, 760 F.2d 1006 (1985).
6.	1981	Jim Walter Corp. v. FTC, 625 F.2d 676 (1980).
7.	1981	In Interest of K.G., 295 N.W.2d 323 (1980).
8.	1983	McNutt v. Superior Court, 648 P.2d 122 (1982).
9.	1981	St. Helen's Farm, (1981) 11 A.T.R. 544.
10.	1985	In re Marriage of Washburn, 677 P.2d 152 (1984).

PART IV. Using LegalTrac, locate and give the citation for a periodical article for each of the following:

Questions:

	Year	Case
1.	1982	John A. Hall Construction Co. v. Boone & Darr, Inc., 302 N.W.2d 850 (1981).
2.	1986	City of Austin v. Mavis, 468 N.E.2d 584 (1984).
3.	1983	In re IBM, 687 F.2d 591 (1982).
4.	1980	R. v. Adams (1980) All E.R. 473.
5.	1980	St. Alexis Hospital v. Eckert, 284 N.W.2d 441 (1979).
6.	1982	In re Marriage of Allen, 626 P.2d 16 (1981).

7.	1982	Estate of Bahen v. United States, 305 F.2d 827 (1962).
8.	1985	Tiffany Fine Arts Inc. v. United States, No. 83-1007 (U.S. Jan. 9, 1985).
9.	1984	McKay v. Davis, 653 P.2d 860 (1982).
10.	1984	Bailey Estate v. Commissioner, 81 T.C. 246 (1983).

ASSIGNMENT 3
LOCATING BOOK REVIEWS THROUGH THE INDEX TO LEGAL PERIODICALS, CURRENT LAW INDEX, LEGAL RESOURCE INDEX AND LEGALTRAC

PART I.

Method:

Using the Index to Legal Periodicals, locate and cite the first review of a book in the calendar year indicated.

	Year Reviewed	Author and Title
1.	1970	Mitford, Jessica, Trial of Dr. Spock.
2.	1970	Report and Recommendations on Disruption of the Judicial Process.
3.	1966	Kalven, Harry, American Jury.
4.	1968	Keeton, Robert, After Cars Crash.
5.	1963	Mental Illness and Due Process.
6.	1975	Schwartz, Bernard, Law in America: A History.
7.	1972	Rawls, John, Theory of Justice (1971).
8.	1973	Dobbs, Dan B., Handbook on the Law of Remedies (1973).
9.	1967	Uniform System of Citation (1967).
10.	1969	Keeton, Robert E., Venturing to Do Justice (1969).
11.	1966	Cavers, David F., Choice-of-Law Process (1965).
12.	1972	First Report of the National Commission on Marihuana and Drug Abuse (1972).
13.	1970	Clark, Ramsey, Crime in America (1970).
14.	1971	Swartz, Edward, Toys that Don't Care (1971).
15.	1972	Pentagon Papers (1971).
16.	1972	Aerial Piracy and International Law (1971).

17.	1969	Chapman, Dennis, Sociology and the Stereotype of the Criminal (1968).
18.	1970	Clor, Harry M., Obscenity and Public Morality (1969).
19.	1965	Young, Leontine R., Wednesday's Children: A Study of Child Neglect and Abuse (1964).
20.	1972	Brown, Kent, Medical Problems and the Law (1971).

PART II. Using Current Law Index, locate, cite and give grade for the review of a book in the periodical and calendar year indicated.

Questions:

	Year	Periodical	Author and Title
1.	1984	American Bar Foundation Research Journal	Best, Arthur, When Consumers Complain.
2.	1981	Duke Law Journal	Shapo, Marshall S., A Nation of Guinea Pigs.
3.	1984	Commercial Law Journal	Friedman, Milton R. Friedman on Leases, 2d ed.
4.	1984	Harvard Law Review	Blasi, Vincent, The Burger Court: The Counter-Revolution That Wasn't.
5.	1984	Yale Law Journal	Ackerman, Bruce, Reconstructing American Law.
6.	1984	Harvard Law Review	Epstein, Cynthia, Women in Law.
7.	1984	Wisconsin Law Review	Bickel, Alexander M., The Judiciary and Responsible Government 1910-1921.
8.	1984	Harvard Law Review	Christie, George, Law, Norms and Authority.
9.	1983	Harvard Law Review	Stevens, Robert, Law School: Legal Education in America from the 1850's to the 1980's.
10.	1984	American Journal of Jurisprudence	Schauer, Frederick, Free Speech: A Philosophical Inquiry.

Chapter 17

PART III. Using Legal Resource Index, locate, cite and give grade for the review of a book in the periodical and calendar year indicated.

Questions:

	Year	Periodical	Author and Title
1.	1983	Texas Law Review	Wright, Charles Alan, The Law of Federal Courts, 4th ed.
2.	1984	Criminal Law Bulletin	Trillin, Calvin, Killings.
3.	1982	Cornell Law Review	Tushnet, Mark V., The American Law of Slavery.
4.	1985	California Law Review	Simpson, A. W. Brian, Cannibalism and the Common Law.
5.	1981	Boston College International and Comparative Law Review	Murphy, Earl Finbar, Energy and Environmental Balance.
6.	1983	Supreme Court Law Review	Hirsch, H. N., The Enigma of Felix Frankfurter.
7.	1986	Los Angeles Daily Journal	Dworkin, Ronald, Law's Empire.
8.	1986	University of Chicago Law Review	Epstein, Richard A., Takings: Private Property and the Power of Eminent Domain.
9.	1983	Trial	Alexander, Shana, Very Much a Lady: The Untold Story of Jean Harris and Dr. Herman Tarnower.
10.	1980	Michigan Law Review	White, G. Edward, Patterns of American Legal Thought.

PART IV. Using LegalTrac, locate, cite and give grade for the review of a book in the periodical and calendar year indicated.

Questions:

	Year	Periodical	Author and Title
1.	1983	Temple Law Quarterly	Dershowitz, Alan M., The Best Defense.
2.	1985	Los Angeles Daily Journal	Coleman, Jonathan, At

			Mother's Request: A True Story of Money, Murder and Betrayal.
3.	1984	Georgia Law Review	White, James Boyd, When Words Lose Their Meaning: Constitutions and Reconstructions of Language, Character and Community.
4.	1985	American Journal of Legal History	Schwartz, Bernard, Super Chief: Earl Warren and His Supreme Court.
5.	1982	Yale Law Journal	Calabresi, Guido, A Common Law for the Age of Statutes.
6.	1985	Columbia Law Review	Posner, Richard, The Federal Courts: Crisis and Reform.
7.	1985	Louisiana Law Review	Kennedy, Duncan, Legal Education and the Reproduction of Hierarchy: A Polemic Against the System.
8.	1981	Harvard Law Review	Simon, James F., Independent Journey.
9.	1986	American Bar Journal	Johnstone, Quintin, Paralegals--Progress and Prospects of a Satellite Occupation.
10.	1982	Justice System Journal	Stolz, Preble, Judging Judges: The Investigation of Rose Bird and the California Supreme Court.

ASSIGNMENT 4
PROBLEM APPROACH TO FINDING PERIODICAL ARTICLES

PART I. Using Index to Legal Periodicals, answer the following:

Questions:

1. Find a 1966 article concerned with attitudes toward the Los Angeles race riot.

2. Locate a case involving a prisoner's rights under the Federal Tort Claims Act, and a 1955 law review comment thereon.

3. Find a 1973 discussion of insuring the condominium.

4. Find a 1971 article on the rule against perpetuities and the spendthrift trust in New York.

5. Cite a 1960 note on the common law liability of liquor vendors.

6. Find a 1973 article concerned with discrimination against women in the extension of credit.

7. Locate a 1967 article on blood transfusions where an adult Jehovah's Witness is involved.

8. Locate a 1969 note calling for legislation to protect computer programs.

9. Cite a 1955 and 1956 article (printed two places) concerned with the fingerprinting of bar applicants.

10. Cite a 1968 model movie censorship ordinance.

11. Find a 1974 article concerned with airline "bumping" and baggage loss.

12. Cite a 1952 article concerned with the U.S. General Accounting Office's right to inspect government contractors' records.

13. Find a 1966 article on the malpractice of psychiatrists.

14. Locate an article discussing a (1959) case involving negligence for animals on the highway as a cause of motor vehicle accident.

15. Find a survey of the work of the U.S. Court of Appeals for the Sixth Circuit for the year 1971-72.

16. Locate a 1955 article on the drafting of a book publishing contract.

17. Find a 1957 article concerned with the origin of credit life insurance.

18. Cite a 1971 article on computer program protection.

19. Find a 1975 article dealing with live organ transplants from minor donors in Massachusetts.

20. Cite a 1967 article discussing slumlordism as a tort.

PART II. Using Current Law Index, answer the following:

Questions:

1. Cite a 1980 article on tax collection policies and practices.

2. Locate a 1981 article on rethinking rent control in New Jersey.

3. Find a 1982 article on community property taxation and joint and several federal income tax liability.

4. Locate an article from 1983 discussing federal injunctions and the public interest.

5. Find a 1984 article on whether automated tellers at groceries constitute branch banking.

6. Find a 1984 article about the role of religion in the public school curriculum.

7. Cite a 1985 article suggesting tort damages for fear and risk of injury.

8. Locate a 1985 article on modifying U.S. acceptance of the compulsory jurisdiction of the World Court.

9. Find a 1985 speech on the private management of asbestos litigation.

10. Cite a 1985 discussion of taking voting rights seriously.

PART III. Using Legal Resource Index, answer the following:

Questions:

1. Locate a 1984 article on copyright and the visual artists' display right.

2. Cite a 1981 article on the religion clauses of the First Amendment.

3. Locate a 1986 article on the definition and regulation of nursing homes.

4. Cite a 1986 article which tells law students how to cope with rejection.

5. Find a 1983 article on the limits and dangers of environmental mediation.

6. Find a 1984 article that is an economic inquiry into law firm profit sharing.

7. Locate a 1985 article giving a history of Massachusetts and its judges.

8. Find a 1985 article on the automation of legal research discussing whether LEXIS and WESTLAW make legal research easier.

9. Cite a 1985 article discussing employment discrimination against persons with AIDS.

10. Locate a 1984 article on genetic counseling and screening.

PART IV. Using LegalTrac, answer the following:

Questions:

1. Cite a 1983 discussion of the use and abuse of liquidated damages in federal defense contracts.

2. Locate a 1986 bibliography on gun control.

3. Find a 1986 article about AIDS in the workplace.

4. Cite a 1984 article explaining resolving civil disputes in a church environment.

5. Find a 1985 article which gives the English perspective on the American abortion debate.

6. Locate a 1984 discussion of commercial paper as "security" under the Glass-Steagall Act.

7. Locate a 1986 article explaining New York's new rules for handling asbestos.

8. Find a 1985 article on job burnout among narcotics investigators.

9. Find a 1986 article on the role of in-vitro fertilization in the treatment of infertility.

10. Cite a 1986 explanation of why the Treasury dropped its 20-year bonds.

CHAPTER 18

TREATISES, RESTATEMENTS, MODEL CODES, AND UNIFORM LAWS

ASSIGNMENT 1
USE OF TORTS TREATISES

Method:

(1) Answer each problem with either a "Yes" or "No" according to the majority view.

(2) Using the source indicated in parentheses find the answers to the following questions. Properly cite the applicable section number and page. For example:

F. Harper & F. James, Jr., & O. Gray The Law of Torts sec. _, at _ (2d ed. 1986).

Prosser and Keeton on the Law of Torts sec. _, at _ (5th ed. 1984).

(3) Properly cite the cases or other materials as requested.

Questions:

1. Can loud noises constitute an actionable private nuisance? Cite a law review article on point cited in a footnote. (Prosser and Keeton)

2. May a woman bring an action in battery for being kissed without her consent? Cite a Missouri case on point. (Harper, James & Gray)

3. Does a person have a right to dynamite a house if this is necessary to stop the spread of a conflagration that threatens a town? Cite a California case on point. (Prosser and Keeton)

4. May a child maintain an action for the consequences of prenatal injuries? Cite a 1951 New York case on point. (Harper, James & Gray)

5. Is it necessary for a person to be physically restrained in order to bring an action for false imprisonment? Cite a 1924 Maryland case on point. (Prosser and Keeton)

6. If, without negligence, a person cuts down a tree on his own land and it falls on adjoining land, does the adjoining landowner have a cause of action? Cite an 1841 North Carolina case on point. (Prosser and Keeton)

7. Does an experienced baseball spectator have a cause of action if he is injured by a batted ball while attending a baseball game? Cite a Washington case on point. (Harper, James & Gray)

8. Is "hostile intent" the gist of an action of battery? (Prosser and Keeton)

9. May damages be awarded for mental distress suffered at the hands of a practical joker? Cite an English case on point. (Harper, James & Gray)

10. May an insane person be held liable for wrongful death? Cite a 1887 case on point. (Prosser and Keeton)

11. May a father be held liable for the damage caused by his son's negligent driving of the family car? Cite a 1915 Georgia case on point. (Harper, James & Gray)

12. May a funeral parlor located in a residential community be considered a private nuisance? Cite a Michigan case holding that a nuisance exists. (Prosser and Keeton)

13. Can a defendant who engages in blasting activities within city limits be held strictly liable for concussion damages? Cite a 1963 Indiana case on point. (Prosser and Keeton)

14. Should a minor engaged in driving an automobile be held to the same standard of care as an adult? Cite a 1981 Minnesota case on point. (Prosser and Keeton)

15. Does the erroneous dissemination of a credit rating by a credit rating bureau, falsely alleging an account was overdue, constitute defamation? Cite a 1918 Florida case on point. (Harper, James & Gray)

16. Are police and firemen deemed invites rather than licensees when summoned to a public place in the line of duty? Cite a 1974 Nebraska case on point relating to police. (Prosser and Keeton)

17. Is an insane person held to the same standard of conduct as that required of a sane person? Cite a 1905 law review article on point. (Prosser and Keeton)

18. Does a municipality enjoy the same sovereign immunity as the state? Cite the original 1788 case on point. (Harper, James & Gray)

19. Is an ordinary man free to act in reliance upon the opinion of an expert jeweler as to the value of a diamond? Cite a 1862 Michigan case a point. (Prosser and Keeton)

20. Does the physician's standard of conduct differ from that of the reasonable man in general? Cite a 1959 law review article. (Prosser and Keeton)

21. In a civil action for damages against more than one person, are all of the defendants who acted in concert equally liable? Cite a 1920 Minnesota case on point. (Prosser and Keeton)

22. Is owner of a known vicious watchdog liable for damages if the dog attacks a trespasser who has not been warned of the dog's presence? Cite a 1837 New York case on point. (Harper, James & Gray)

23. Is a credit agency, such as a mutual credit organization, liable for defamation of character of a person as a bad credit risk if made in good faith? Cite a 1959 California case on point. (Prosser and Keeton)

24. Has there been a false arrest where a woman's purse was taken from her as security so that she would not leave a store? Cite a 1946 Kentucky case on point. (Prosser and Keeton)

25. Is the owner of a leopard responsible for injury it may cause? Cite a 1919 California case on point. (Harper, James & Gray)

26. Is it considered trespass to mine under adjoining land? Cite a 1863 California case on point. (Harper, James & Gray)

27. Does an automobile manufacturer give an implied warranty as to the safety of his product? Cite the leading 1960 case and the classic periodical article which traced subsequent development of the principle. (Prosser and Keeton)

28. Is snatching a newspaper out of another person's hand sufficient to satisfy the elements of battery? Cite an Illinois case on point. (Harper, James & Gray)

29. Is a person in charge of a restaurant privileged to retain for thirty minutes a customer he suspects may not have paid his bill? Cite an 1873 Massachusetts case on point. (Harper, James & Gray)

30. Is a child liable for torts such as slander of defamation of another? Cite a 1898 Missouri case on point. (Harper, James & Gray)

ASSIGNMENT 2
USE OF CONTRACTS TREATISES

Method:

(1) Answer each problem with either a "Yes" or "No" according to the majority view.

(2) Using the source indicated in the parentheses, find the answers to the following questions. Properly cite the applicable section number and page. For example:

A. Corbin on Contracts sec. _, at _ (multi-volume edition).

S. Williston, A Treatise on the Law of Contracts sec. _, at _ (3d ed.).

(3) Properly cite the cases or other materials as requested in the problems.

Questions:

1. May the winner of a bet judicially recover money from a wager which was won where the money was not paid? Cite a Louisiana case on point. (Corbin or Williston)

2. May a department store advertise well-known brands of radios at reduced prices without being held to have made an offer? Cite a New York case on point. (Corbin)

3. May a person claim a reward for the return of lost property if he had no prior knowledge of the existence of such reward? Cite a District of Columbia case on point. (Corbin or Williston)

4. Does a marriage constitute sufficient consideration to support contractual promise? Cite an Ohio case on point. (Corbin)

5. Does failure of an instalment purchaser to pay for an instalment excuse the seller from delivering later instalment? Cite a 1925 federal case on point. (Corbin)

6. Must a memorandum in writing be written in ink to satisfy the statute? Cite a New York case on point. (Corbin)

7. Does a statement on the face on an instrument that it has been executed in pursuance of a specified contract satisfy the Negotiable Instruments Law? Cite a North Carolina case on point. (Corbin)

8. May one make a gift of money by giving another his savings account passbook? Cite a Michigan case on point. (Williston)

9. Is a barred action for a tort revived by a new promise to pay? cite a Washington case on point. (Corbin)

10. Is a credit card holder responsible for purchases made by a thief who uses such credit card? Cite an Oregon case on point. (Williston)

11. If a farmer buys a specific type of seed warranted to grow a certain crop, and the seed grows another crop, is that farmer entitled to the full value of the warranted crop? Cite a leading New York case. (Corbin)

12. Will the courts enforce the promise of a window to pay the debts of her deceased husband? Cite a North Carolina case on point. (Corbin)

13. May a contract be accepted by the act of dropping a letter of acceptance into a mail box? Cite an Iowa case on point. (Corbin)

14. Does the fall of the hammer at an auction constitute the acceptance of a contract? Cite an Illinois case on point. (Williston)

15. If a document has been properly sealed and delivered, will it also require a signature in order to be valid? Cite an Arkansas case on point. (Williston)

16. May the renting of the upper story apartment unit to a college fraternity be sufficient reason for the tenant below to claim constructive eviction? Cite a 1926 Wisconsin case on point. (Corbin)

17. Can the estate of a mural painter be sued for damages because the painter died and could not fulfill the contract himself? Cite a 1930 New York case on point. (Corbin)

18. Will a court enforce an indefinite contract which provided one party a division of the profits "upon a very liberal basis?" Cite a 1907 Pennsylvania case on point. (Corbin)

19. Can an audition seller contract with a "puffer" to make false bids on items in order to drive up the price? Cite a 1926 Kentucky case on point. (Corbin)

20. Must the subject of a portrait pay an artist for painting a portrait whereby payment was to occur only if the painting satisfied the artistic taste and personal fancy of the subject? Cite a 1878 Michigan case on point. (Corbin)

21. Can an airline or other common carrier bargain to render service for a price and at the same time provide for exemption from liability for its negligence? Cite a 1944 federal case on point. (Corbin)

22. Does dishonesty (e.g., accepting gifts from seller for buying from him) on the part of an employee terminate a contract of employment at the opinion of the employer? Cite a Missouri case on point. (Corbin)

23. Has "Bank Night" at a movie theatre ever been held to be an illegal lottery? Cite a Georgia case on point. (Corbin)

24. Is a real estate broker entitled to receive his sales commission if he locates a buyer at the agreed price and the owner then refuses to make a conveyance upon the agreed terms? Cite an Alabama case on point. (Corbin)

25. Can the offer of a sizable reward by display of a poster be revoked by simply removing the poster? Cite an Iowa case on point. (Corbin)

26. Can a company refuse to honor a "contract" made by one of its salesmen when every saleman's order pad has printed on it: "All contracts and orders are subject to the approval of the home office," though this statement has not been specifically called to the attention of the buyer? Cite a 1915 New York case on point. (Corbin)

27. Can a school board contract with a teacher to employ her for a specified limited period of time on condition that she shall remain unmarried during such period? Cite an Ohio case on point. (Corbin).

28. Can a murderer recover on an insurance policy if he is named as the beneficiary? Cite a Supreme Court case a point. (Williston)

29. Is a drunkard's contract voidable? Cite a North Dakota case on point. (Williston)

30. Can a minor who has by bond or contract agreed to support his bastard child avoid his transaction? Cite an Indiana case on point. (Williston)

ASSIGNMENT 3
USE OF A.L.I. RESTATEMENTS

Method:

(1) Answer each problem with either a "Yes" or "No".

(2) Referring to either Restatement (Second) of Contracts (1979) or Restatement (Second) of Torts (first 2 vols.) (1964), give the applicable section number of the Restatement volume where the answer was found.

(3) Cite cases on point under applicable section headings in the following volumes:

Restatement in the Courts, 1970-71 Supplement, 1971-73 Supplement, or 1984-85 Supplement.

Restatement (Second) of Torts (Appendix 1964).

Questions:

1. Must a donee beneficiary be identified at the time a contract promise is made in order to have rights under that contract? Cite a 1983 case on point.

2. If one of the remedies for breach of contract is not available to the plaintiff and he in good faith has sought that remedy, will this be a bar to a suit for a different remedy? Cite a 1982 case on point.

3. In a breach of contract action, may damages be awarded for mental suffering in the absence of wanton or reckless action which did not cause bodily harm? Cite a 1982 New York case on point.

4. Is an agreement entered into under coercion voidable? Cite a 1982 case on point.

5. Does a reply to an offer which purports to accept it but adds qualifications constitute an acceptance? Cite a 1982 Nebraska case on point.

6. Is an antenuptial agreement which does not unreasonably encourage divorce void as against public policy? Cite a 1981 Massachusetts case on point.

7. Is a former employee entitled to receive punitive damages from his former employer for breach of an employment contract? Cite a 1983 Virginia case on point.

8. Does bad faith behavior amount to a repudiation of a contract if it does not constitute a failure to provide the other party with goods or services called for in the contract? Cite a 1982 case on point.

9. Will contributory negligence bar recovery in a suit based upon an intentionally inflicted tort? Cite a 1963 Alaska case on point.

10. Can a threat made merely in words constitute an assault? Cite a 1960 Pennsylvania case on point.

11. Is a soldier liable civilly for injury to another which results from following the orders of a superior officer? Cite a 1941 Massachusetts case on point.

12. Will the courts recognize a citizen arrest without a warrant where the citizen-passerby is a witness to the crime which has been committed? Cite a Pennsylvania case on point.

13. Does the granting of permission by a home owner to a canvasser to enter a home make such canvasser an invitee as opposed to a licensee? Cite a 1919 Washington case on point.

14. Does the so-called "reasonable man" standard apply equally to children? Cite a 1934 Connecticut case on point.

15. Is an actor liable for negligent conduct which results in emotional disturbance alone, without bodily harm or other compensable damage? Cite the first A.L.R annotation listed under this section as a cross reference.

16. May one use the same means of self-defense to protect himself against confinement as he may use to protect himself against bodily harm? Cite the Digest System Key Number under this section.

17. Is a common carrier or other public utility liable for gross insults to patrons by its employees? Cite a 1970 California case on point.

18. Was the employer of a contractor who began excavation for construction of a building on a vacant lot responsible for cracks appearing in the wall of a building already on an adjacent lot by virtue of the withdrawal of "lateral support" for such an older building? Cite a 1971 Iowa case on point.

19. Is a person or business liable for "conversion" of a chattel if he alters its physical condition or changes its identity? Cite a 1969 New Hampshire case on point.

20. Does the negligence of a husband or wife bar the other from recovery for his or her physical harm? Cite a 1972 New Hampshire case on point.

ASSIGNMENT 4
DRILL PROBLEMS AND THEME PROBLEMS

Drill Problem I:

A. Using J. Calamari & J. Perillo, The Law of Contracts (3d ed. 1987), answer the following, citing the supporting section and/or case where applicable.

1. Does a sealed contract require consideration?

2. Where can one find a discussion of Patton v. Arney?

B. Using Prosser and Keeton on The Law of Torts (5th ed. 1984), answer the following, citing a supporting section or page where appropriate.

1. Can a child recover for damages due to an injury caused to the mother when pregnant?

2. Have lunatics generally been held liable for their torts?

Drill Problem II:

A. Using J. Calamari & J Perillo, The Law of Contracts (3d ed. 1987), answer the following, citing the supporting section and/or case where applicable:

1. What is the modern definition of duress?

2. Cite a case where an unlicensed milk dealer was allowed to recover despite the fact the services rendered were illegal.

B. Using Prosser and Keeton on The Law of Torts (5th ed. 1984), answer the following, citing a supporting section or page where appropriate.

1. Does an action lie against a dealer who describes what turns out to be a lemon as a "dandy," a "bearcat" and a "sweet job"? Cite a 1932 Texas case.

2. Where can one find discussion of Clary v. Hale?

3. Does the consent of the plaintiff constitute an absolute privilege to speak without fear of being sued for defamation?

Drill Problem III:

A. Using J. Calamari & J. Perillo, The Law of Contracts (3d ed. 1987), answer the following, citing the supporting section and/or case where applicable.

1. Will a plaintiff be granted equitable relief if he comes to court with "unclean" hands?

2. Where can one find mention of Continental Illinois Bank & Trust

Co. v. Clement?

B. Using Prosser and Keeton on The Law of Torts (5th ed. 1984), answer the following, citing a supporting section or page where appropriate.

1. At common law could the wife sue for interference with domestic relations?

2. When did the special rule as to injuries to children who are hurt while trespassing first appear in the United States?

3. Does revenge qualify as a defense to intentional assault?

Theme Problem I:

A. Roe v. Wade dealt with constitutional issues of privacy. Using L. Tribe, American Constitutional Law (2d ed. 1988), answer the following. Put your answers in Blue Book form.

1. List the first three places that Roe v. Wade is discussed.

2. Who was the first President to invoke executive privilege?

3. On what date was the Equal Rights Amendment passed by Congress? Where does the text of the amendment appear?

B. Using J. Nowak, R. Rotunda & J. Young, Constitutional Law (3d ed. 1986), answer the following, putting your answer in Blue Book form.

1. Give the first two places that Roe v. Wade is discussed.

2. May a state eliminate the teaching of certain ideas because they conflict with certain religious beliefs?

3. What Edmund Wilson novel was adjudged obscene?

C. Is there a restatement on Constitutional Law?

CHAPTER 20

RESEARCH IN INTERNATIONAL LAW

ASSIGNMENT 1
PRE-1950 UNITED STATES TREATIES AND INTERNATIONAL AGREEMENTS

Sources:

Treaties in Force, 1989

Treaties and Other International Agreements of the United States of America, 1776-1949, by Charles E. Bevans;

United States Treaties and Other International Agreeements Cumulative Index, 1776-1949, compiled by Igor I. Kavass and Mark A. Michael; and

Shepard's United States Citations, Statute Edition, for part 5 of each question.

Method:

Give the following for each treaty or international agreement listed below:

(1) Its citation in Statutes at Large and concurrent citation in Bevans' Treaties (if any), for example, 43 Stat. 1621, 6 Bevans 1033;

(2) Its date or dates of signature, opening for signature, exchange of notes, etc. (but not the dates of ratification, proclamation, or entry into force), for example, Nov. 10, 1922; and

(3) Its E.A.S., T.S., or T.I.A.S. number, for example, T.S. No. 668.

(4) Is it in force? If so, give the date of its entry into force. Also give year and page reference to the 1989 edition of Treaties in Force containing this information, for example, April 27, 1923, 1989 T.I.F. 36.

(5) Its subsequent judicial, legislative, or diplomatic developments (if any), as shown in Shepard's United States Citations, Statute Edition 1986. Copy as appearing in Shepard's, for example, 29OUS294, 78LE324, 54SC105.

The easiest way to determine the answer to questions (1), (2), (3), and (4) is to first check Treaties in Force. If you do not find the answer in Treaties in Force, check the index to the Bevans work or the Kavass, Michael Index.

Treaties in Force, though not the best index ever produced, is easy to use. It has two main divisions: Part 1 for bilateral treaties and agreements between the United States and other countries or political entities and Part 2 for multilateral treaties and agreements. Part 1 is arranged alphabetically by country, with subject entries under each country. Territories of a country are placed at the end of that country. Part 2 is arranged alphabetically by subject.

The weakness of Treaties in Force is the choice and number of subject headings and the inadequate use of cross references. However, once you determine if the treaty or agreement is bilateral or multilateral, you can usually find the answer. If bilateral and you know the country, you can quickly scan the appropriate or related subject headings under the country in Part 1 and determine whether the treaty or agreement is in force. If the treaty or agreement is multilateral, you can determine whether it is in force by scanning the appropriate correlated subject headings in Part 2.

If the treaty or agreement is not listed in Treaties in Force, the quickest way to find it is to search the index volume to Bevans' work. This will lead you directly to the answer. You can also search the Kavass, Michael Cumulative Index. The advantage of the former is that it leads you directly to the text in the appropriate Bevans volume.

You can answer question (5) by Shepardizing the citation in Shepard's United States Citation--Statute Edition, 1986.

Questions:

1. Commerce and Navigation Treaty with Turkey
2. Treaty of Arbitration with Estonia, 1930
3. Agreement with Canada to raise the level of Lake St. Francis
4. Parcel post agreement with Bahamas, 1936
5. Treaty establishing friendly relations with Hungary, 1921
6. Agreement with Norway relating to customs treatment of importations for consular offices
7. Agreement with Sweden for exemption of pleasure yachts from navigation dues.
8. Provisional agreement about commerce with Egypt
9. Treaty of arbitration with Sweden
10. Treaty about traveling salesmen with Venezuela
11. Extradition treaty with Costa Rica
12. Fuel and vegetable oil agreement with Argentina

13. Exchange of official publications with Brazil

14. Agreement relative to postal money orders in Postal Union of the Americas and Spain, 1936

15. Agricultural experiment station agreement with Ecuador, 1942

16. Military obligations agreement with Finland

17. Agreement for "Haitinization" with Haiti

18. Rights of U.S. in Iraq

19. Proclamation of copyright extension with Australia, 1949

20. Agreement for maritime claims and litigation with France

ASSIGNMENT 2
POST-1950 UNITED STATES TREATIES AND INTERNATIONAL AGREEMENTS

Sources: Treaties in Force, 1989;

Cumulative Index to United States Treaties and Other International Agreements, 1950-1970, compiled by Igor I. Kavass and Adolf Sprudzs; and

Shepard's United States Citations, Statute Edition, for Part (5) of each question.

Method:

Give the following for each treaty or international agreement listed below:

(1) Its citation in United States Treaties and Other International Agreements, for example, 12 U.S.T. 908;

(2) Its date or dates of signature, opening for signature, exchange of notes, etc. (but not the dates of ratification, proclamation, or entry into force), for example, Oct. 1, 1951; and

(3) Its T.I.A.S. number, for example, T.I.A.S. No. 4797.

(4) Is it in force? If so, the date of its entry into force. Also give year and page references to the 1989 edition of Treaties in Force containing this information, for example, July 30, 1961, 1989 T.I.F. 40.

(5) Its subsequent judicial, legislative, or diplomatic developments (if any), as shown in Shepard's United States Citations, Statute Edition, 1986. Copy as appearing in Shepard's, for example, 297FS349.

The easiest way to determine the answer to questions (1), (2), (3), and (4) is to first check Treaties in Force. (See the explanation for the use of Treaties in Force under Assignment 1.) If you do not find the answer in Treaties in Force, check the appropriate volume of the Kavass and Sprudzs work. Volumes 3, Country, and 4, Subject, will, in most cases, supply the answer if Treaties in Force does not.

You can answer question (5) by Shepardizing the citation in Shepard's United States Citations--Statute Edition, 1986.

Questions:

1. Economic cooperation ageement with France, 1950 amendment

2. Economic cooperation agreement with Italy, 1950 amendment
3. U.S. Educational Commission agreement with Korea, 1950
4. Multilaterial agreement concerning the prewar external debt of the German Reich
5. Agreement with United Kingdom concerning civil airport facilities in Bermuda, 1951
6. Agreement concerning administration of income tax in Canada of U.S. Government employees in Canada
7. Agreement with Korea concerning mutual security assurances
8. Agreement with Thailand concerning the U.S. Educational Foundation, 1953
9. Agreement with Brazil for a military advisory mission, 1952
10. Agreement with Italy concerning surplus agricultural commodities, March, 1957
11. Multilateral General Agreement on Tariffs and Trade -- eighth protocol of supplementary concessions, 1957
12. Agreement with Korea concerning atomic energy cooperation for civil uses, 1958 amendment
13. Agreement with Italy concerning loan of vessel, 1959
14. International telecommunication convention, Malaga-Torremolinos, 1973
15. Guarantee of private investments agreement with Afghanistan, 1957
16. Agency for the Safety of Air Navigation in Africa and Madagascar
17. Double taxation agreement with Argentina concerning the operation of ships and aircraft
18. Agreement concerning participation of Belgian Armed Forces in United Nations Operations in Korea
19. Peace Corps agreement with Bolivia, 1962
20. Conventiion for the exchange of postal money orders with the colony of British Virgin Islands

ASSIGNMENT 3
UNITED NATIONS TREATY SERIES
(CHRONOLOGICAL INDEX)

Source: United Nations Treaty Series Cumulative Index, Nos. 1-9 (covering volumes 1-650 of United Nations Treaty Series).

Method:

By using the Chronological Index, give the following for each of the treaties listed below:

(1) The U.N.T.S. number, e.g. I:7999; and

(2) The U.N.T.S. volume and page number where the text of the treaty may be found, e.g. 549 U.N.T.S. 173.

The answers to these problems are relatively easy to find. You have only to locate the date of the treaty concerned in the Chronological Index of the appropriate Cumulative Index volumes. You may have to look in several different volumes, however, to find the date of the treaty or agreement in question.

Questions:

1. Charter of the Organization of American States, April 30, 1948

2. Agreement between Italy and the Netherlands about free assistance before the courts for indigents and waiver of security costs, January 9, 1884

3. An exchange of notes between Luxemburg and the Netherlands on freedom of the air for regular international air services, April 14, 1948

4. Agreement between Hungary and Soviet Union on mutual legal assistance in matters relating to the temporary presence of Soviet forces on Hungarian territory, April 24, 1958

5. Multipartite agreement for research on the effects of radioactivity in the sea, March 8/10, 1961

6. Agreement between Austria and Soviet Union concerning settlement of the technical and commercial questions relating to navigation of the Danube, June 14, 1957

7. Loan to Norway by Canada of three frigates, December 20, 1955

8. Exchange of notes between Columbia and the United States on the service of nationals of one country in the armed forces of the other, January 27/February 12, 1944

9. Multipartite agreement of armistice with Bulgaria, October 28, 1944

10. General agreement of technical cooperation between Egypt and the United States, May 5, 1951

11. Trade agreement between India and Burma, September 29, 1951

12. Agreement for health projects in Korea, September 19, 1951

13. Commercial agreement between France and Greece, December 23, 1952

14. Air transport agreement between Luxemburg and Iceland, October 23, 1952

15. The Brussels Treaty for collaboration in economic, social, and cultural matters, March 17, 1948

16. Manila accord, July 31, 1963

17. Agreement between Canada and France on films and film production, October 11, 1963

18. Nordic mutual emergency assistance agreement, October 17, 1963

19. Agreement between Netherlands and Nigeria for the development of the Faculty of Engineering at the University of Nigeria, Nsukku, December 4, 1964

20. Trade agreement between Australia and Philippines, June 16, 1965

21. Consular convention between Finland and Soviet Union, January 24, 1966

22. Exchange of notes on the use of seamen's books as travel documents, June 15/20, 1967

23. Exchange of notes on abolition of visas between Austria and Dominican Republic, February 21, 1968

24. Treaty of friendship between Gabon and Israel, May 15, 1962

25. Monetary agreement between Switzerland and the United Kingdom, March 12, 1946

ASSIGNMENT 4
UNITED NATIONS TREATY SERIES
(ALPHABETICAL INDEX)

Source: United Nations Treaty Series Cumulative Index, Nos. 1-9 (covering volumes 1-650 of United Nations Treaty Series).

Method:

By using the Alphabetical Index, give the following for each treaty described below:

(1) The U.N.T.S. number, e.g. I:7741; and

(2) The U.N.T.S. volume and page number where the text of the treaty may be found, e.g. 533 U.N.T.S. 157.

As in the preceding set of questions, the answers to these are relatively easy to find. You have only to locate the correct heading in the Alphabetical Index of the appropriate Cumulative Index volume. The Alphabetical Index has four types of major headings: (1) Countries and Organizations, (2) Subjects, (3) General International Agreements (entered under this heading), and (4) Multipartite Instruments (entered under this heading). All four types are listed in the Alphabetical Index. Most of the answers can be found under the names of the countries in question, but you may have to search in several volumes before finding the answer.

Questions:

1. Agreement to avoid double taxation and to prevent fiscal evasion between Finland and Israel, January 21, 1965

2. Agreement to exchange information on mental patients between the Netherlands and West Germany, July 13 and 18, 1961

3. An agreement of cultural cooperation between Poland and Mongolia, December 23, 1958

4. Agreement to permit Faroese fishermen to engage in hand line fishing off the coast of Iceland and Denmark, August 1, 1961

5. A multipartite agreement to issue to war-disabled veterans an international book of vouchers for repair of prosthetic and orthopaedic appliances, December 17, 1962

6. Transfer to the USSR of part of Finland, February 3, 1947

7. War damage claims agreement between Italy and United States, March 29, 1957

8. India and Pakistan agreement about the recovery of abducted persons, May 8, 1954

9. Agreement between Italy and Australia about the graves of Italian soldiers buried in Austrialia, August 27, 1953

10. Agreement to protect frontier forests against fire between Argentina and Chile, December 29, 1961

11. United States-Canadian settlement by arbitration of claims relating to Gut Dam, March 25, 1965

12. Swedish-Danish agreement about Swedish fish landings in Denmark, December 5, 1967

13. Czechoslovakia Mongolian cooperation on quarantine of plants and their protection against pests, diseases, and weeds, December 9, 1966

14. Agreement between the United Kingdom and Cameroon for interest free loan towards modernizing Cameroon's telecommunication system, June 16, 1967

15. Agreement between Canada and Bolivia on exchange of messages for third parties by amateur radio stations, May 31, 1963

16. Agreement between Canada and Italy on sale of waste materials and scrap belonging to Royal Canadian Air Force, December 18, 1961

17. Supplement of September 18, 1963 to the agreement between Canada and Italy about the sale of waste materials and scrap belonging to Royal Canadian Air Force, September 18, 1963

18. Netherlands-Germany settlement of frontier questions, April 8, 1960

19. Agreement between Romania and Yugoslavia on compensation for damages caused by the construction of the Iron Gates water power and navigation system on the Danube, November 30, 1963

20. Agreement between Netherlands and Ecuador on establishment of a dairy farming training center and modernization of technique of slaughtering cattle for consumption in Ecuador, January 14, 1965

21. Agreement between the United States and Vietnam on television broadcasting in Vietnam, January 3, 1966

22. Agreement between the United Kingdom and Greece for restoration of land on which Anglo-French Crimean War Cemetery at New Phaleron is situated, December 17, 1965-January 12, 1966

23. Service of national contingent provided by Finland with United Nations Peace-Keeping Force in Cyprus, February 21, 1966

24. Agreement between the United States and Ireland for the use of counterpart of special account for a scholarship exchange program, March 16, 1957

25. Agreement between Hungary and Iraq on cooperation in radio, television, cinema, theater, and news, October 11, 1961

ASSIGNMENT 5
GENERAL TREATIES

Sources:

Cumulative Index. United Nations Treaty Series

General Index. League of Nations Treaty Series

Parry, C., Consolidated Treaty Series, 1969, and

Parry, C., Index Guide to Treaties, based on the Consolidated Treaty Series, General Chronological List 1648-1809.

Method:

By using the above indexes and, when called for, consulting the treaty itself, answer the questions below. When a cite is called for, give either the United Nations or League of Natiions Treaty Series volume and page number or the volume and page of treaty given in the Consolidated Treaty Series, for example, 364 U.N.T.S. 3, 25 L.N.T.S. 12, 1 C.T.S. 271.

Please note that the U.N.T.S. and the L.N.T.S. indexes are divided into chronological and alphabetical sections.

Questions:

1. Where can a copy of the Capitulation of Yorktown, 1781 (Generals Washington and Cornwallis) be found?

2. Is Upper Volta a signatory to the African Migratory Locust Convention of 1962? Is Zaire?

3. Where can a copy of the Locarno Pact of 1925 (treaty of mutual guarantee final protocol) be found?

4. Is the agreement establishing the Asian Coconut Community (1968) in force? Has the Philippines ratified it?

5. Where can a copy of the Treaty of Amity, Conciliation, and Arbitration between Italy and Ethiopia (Abyssinia), 1928, be found?

6. During 1963 what nations ratified the European Convention on Academic Recognition of University Qualifications, Dec. 14, 1959?

7. Where can a copy of the agreement between the Free City of Danzig with Germany, Great Britain, Denmark, Poland, and Sweden, 1929, on the regulation of plaice and flounder fishing in the Baltic Sea be found?

8. Where can a copy of the Peace of Westphalia, 1648 (two parts), be found?

9. Cite best source for a list of the denunciations made in 1952 of the Convention for the Safety of Life at Sea, May 31, 1929

10. Where can a copy of the Tokyo Agreement of February 19, 1954 on status of U.N. forces in Japan be found?

11. Where can a copy of the Polish/Democratic Republic of Korea Cultural Cooperation Treaty of 1956 be found?

12. Where can a copy of the Mutual Assistance Treaty, Poland-Great Britain, 1939, be found?

13. Where can a copy of the Agreement Abolishing Visas, Israel-Austria, 1968, be found?

14. Where can a copy of the Treaty Between the U.S. and the Sioux Indians, 1851, be found?

15. Where can a copy of the Buraimi Oasis Arbitration Agreement of 1954 be found?

ASSIGNMENT 6
WHITEMAN'S DIGEST OF INTERNATIONAL LAW

Source: Whiteman, Marjorie M., Digest of International Law (1963-1973)

Method:

Use the index to Whiteman to cite the volume and page references to the topics listed below.

Sample answer: 10:577

Questions:

1. Withdrawal of Cuba from International Monetary Fund
2. Dangerous or humiliating labor for prisoners of war
3. Proof of nationality
4. The right to blockade Suez Canal
5. The legal bases of Arctic (sector principle)
6. Epicontinental sea distinguished from continental shelf: superjacent waters
7. Demilitarization of Aegean Sea islands
8. European Commission of Human Rights
9. Diplomatic status of governments-in-exile
10. Estrada Doctrine
11. The legality of submarine use in war
12. Exclusion of Nazis or Facists from employment in United Nations Secretariat
13. Military air service to Berlin
14. Use of foreign flags by insurgent vessels
15. Seizure of fishing vessels in waters of contested jurisdiction off the coast of Mexico
16. List of treaties and agreements concerning refugees
17. The use of embargo as a means of reprisal

Chapter 20

18. The passage of belligerent warships through the Turkish Straits

19. Repatriation of diplomatic officers in time of war

20. The difference between pillage and booty

21. Harvard draft convention on piracy, 1932

22. Exclusion of Cuba from OAS

23. Legal status of Enderbury Island

24. The use of Shatt-al-Arab River between Iran and Iraq by commercial vessels of all nations

25. The definition of "Hostile Propaganda"

CHAPTER 21

ENGLISH LEGAL RESEARCH

ASSIGNMENT 1
ENGLISH REPORTS, FULL REPRINT

Method:

Using the Index of Cases volumes, provide the English Reports Full Reprint citation for each of the cases cited.

Questions:

1. In re Pugh, 17 Beav. 336.
2. Robinson v. Stone, 2 Strange 1260.
3. Smith v. Dixon, 2 Curt. 264.
4. Wagstaffe v. Bedford, 1 Vern. 95.
5. White's Case, 6 Mod. 18.
6. Price v. Harris, 10 Bing. 331, 557.
7. R. v. Nixon, 1 Strange 185.
8. Smarte v. Edsum, 1 Lev. 30.
9. Gibbon v. Budd, 2 H. & C. 92.
10. Dean v. Abel, Dick. 287.
11. Knox v. Brown, 1 Eq. Rep. 126.
12. Drew v. Coles, 2 C. & J. 505.
13. Buttler v. Mathews, 19 Beav. 549.
14. Aarons v. Williams, 2 Bing. 304.
15. Carter v. Hall, 2 Stark 361.
16. Locke v. Colman, 1 My. & Cr. 423.
17. Jenney v. Brook, 6 Q.B. 323.
18. Lampley v. Blower, 3 Atk. 396.

19. In re The Comet, 5 C. Rob. 285.

20. Wilson v. Millar, 2 Stark. 1

ASSIGNMENT 2
HALSBURY'S LAWS OF ENGLAND, FOURTH EDITION, CASE METHOD

Method:

Locate the citation for each case, using Halsbury's Laws of England (4th ed.). Most cases can be found in the main volumes by using volume 54 (1) and 54 (2), Consolidated Table Cases. If more than one citation is given, cite only the first.

Questions:

1. Adley v. Whitstable.
2. Ashworth v. Browne.
3. A-G v. Prossor.
4. Bane v. Methuen.
5. Allott v. Wagon Repairs.
6. Hudson v. Buck.
7. Guy v. Churchill.
8. Dorset (Duke) v. Crosbie.
9. The Firethorn.
10. Hearn v. Hearn.
11. Clarke v. Barber.
12. Coleman v. North.
13. Ekin v. Flay.
14. Price v. Hall.
15. R. v. Noe.
16. Ashbee v. Jayne.
17. Clarke v. Mumford.
18. Davis v. Rolleston.
19. The Durham City.
20. Dickie v. Singh.

Chapter 21

ASSIGNMENT 3
HALBURY'S LAWS OF ENGLAND, FOURTH EDITION, INDEX METHOD

Method:

Using the Consolidated Index volumes to the Fourth Edition of Halsbury's Laws of England, locate statements in the text which answer each of the following questions. Indicate where this statement was found by citing to the volume and page number of the encyclopedia.

Questions:

1. Did the Highway Acts modify the common law to make it a duty of the highway authorities to light certain roads?
2. Is there a remedy for breach of contract to marry?
3. Can a husband be held criminally liable for the acts of his wife?
4. Is a promoter a trustee or agent of the company he attempts to form?
5. What is the minimum number of persons necessary to form a new company?
6. Can money lent to an illegal company be recovered?
7. May a person accept a revocable offer if it was not made to him?
8. Is a contract void if one party was intoxicated when he or she entered into the contract?
9. Is past consideration a real consideration?
10. Is taking a group picture in front of a sculpture in a museum's foyer a violation of the copyright code?
11. Is a person professing the Jewish religion disqualified from holding the position of Lord Chancellor of Great Britain?
12. May a parent be fined and even imprisoned for failure to comply with a school attendance order?
13. How many kinds of estoppel are there?
14. May a witness be asked leading questions during cross-examination in a criminal case?
15. Is it true that public statutes are judicially noticed and they need not be proved as evidence?
16. There being no special exception, may a young person be

employed on Sunday?

17. May a ferry owner discriminate against certain persons as to use of his ferry?

18. Does the sale of milk containing minute particles of dirt constitute an act of adulteration violative of the food and drug laws?

19. Is there any special restriction for inventions that produce atomic energy?

20. Are prison officers exempt from jury duty?

ASSIGNMENT 4
HALSBBURY'S STATUTES, THIRD EDITION, ALPHABETICAL LIST OF STATUTES

Method:

Using the Tables of Statutes and Index volume of Halsbury's Statutes (3d ed.) to locate the text and annotations to the statute in question. Indicate, by volume and page number, where this statute can be found in this set.

Questions:

1. Act of Supremacy (1558).
2. Admirality Courts Act 1861.
3. Barristers Act 1961.
4. Caravan Sites Act 1968.
5. Children Act 1948.
6. Statute of Westminster 1931.
7. Married Women's Property Act 1964.
8. Bill of Rights (1688).
9. Forcible Entry Act 1381.
10. Union with Ireland Act 1800.
11. Criminal Justice Act 1965.
12. Abortion Act 1967.
13. Firearms Act 1968.
14. Town Development Act 1952.
15. Marriage with Foreigners Act 1906.
16. Colonial Marriages Act 1865.
17. County Courts Act 1924.
18. Cyprus Act 1960.
19. Ecclesiastical Appeals Act 1532.
20. Enemy Property Act 1953.

ASSIGNMENT 5
HALSBURY'S STATUTES, THIRD EDITION, INDEX METHOD

Method:

Use the Table of Statutes and Index volume of Halsbury's Statutes (3d ed.) to find the statutory answers to the following questions. Answer the question and cite Halsbury's Statutes by volume and page.

Questions:

1. What is the age limit for solemnized marriage?
2. In the interpretation of a penal act does the term "person" as stated in such act include corporate bodies?
3. In non-emergency situations how many registered medical practitioners must approve before a pregnancy may be legally terminated?
4. What is the maximum prison term for assaulting a seaman?
5. Is a will witnessed and attested to by only two witnesses valid?
6. Is playing football in the street an offense punishable by fine?
7. In whom is vested the executive power of Canada?
8. Does a husband retain any curtesy right to the estate of his intestate wife?
9. Is martial law permitted?
10. In regard to awarding compensation for riot damage where shall the regulations be published?
11. Must a vehicle being towed show red lights to the side?
12. For the purpose of the law of libel and slander is the broadcasting of words by means of wireless telegraphy permanent publication?
13. For what reason may the local authorities exclude Sue, age 6, from attending the circus?
14. What is the maximum prison term for a second conviction for possession or sale of a flick knife?
15. How many incorporators are necessary in order to form a non-private company?
16. What government official has the duty of causing dangerous fireworks to be destroyed?

17. What is the penalty for contravening the requirement that the keeping of stallions is subject to license or permit?

18. Colossal Condominiums's newest effort is on a disused burial ground. Will they be allowed to build on that location?

19. Does the Constitution of the Board of Architectural Education permit the Cambridge University School of architecture to nominate one person to that Board?

20. Modern Canada was divided into provinces in 1867. two of the provinces, Quebec and Ontario, were derived from two earlier independent provinces. Name these earlier provinces.

21. When did Burma become independent from England?

22. Can a pregnant woman be given a death sentence if she is found guilty of an offense punishable with death?

23. Although the statutes require that the indictment for an act of treason must be processed within three years, there is one treasonous act not bound by this limitation. Name that act.

24. What law guides the penalties for selling fireworks to children?

25. Determine if the Bath Corporation is an authorized undertaker for providing electricity.

ASSIGNMENT 6
HALSBURY'S STATUTES, THIRD EDITION, CURRENT MATERIALS

Method:

Use the 1985 Cumulative Supplement to determine if the indicated statute has been affected by subsequent legislation. Name the subsequent affecting act, if any, and the volume and page number in Halsbury's where it can be located.

Questions:

1. Cockfighting act 1952, Vol. 2, p. 257.
2. Schedule 3 of the Diseases of Animals Act 1950, Vol. 2, p. 372.
3. West Indian Prisons Act 1838, Vol. 4, p. 592.
4. Section 1 of the Administration of Justice (Miscellaneous Provisions) Act 1933, Vol. 8, p. 307.
5. Section 116 of the Education Act 1944, Vol. 11, p. 261.
6. Fireworks Act of 1964, chapter 23, Vol. 13, p. 242.
7. Section 19 Civil Evidence Act 1968, Vol. 12, p. 932.
8. Shop Clubs Act 1902, Vol. 14, p. 329.
9. Guardianship of Infants Act 1886, Vol. 17, p. 415.
10. Section 36 of the Rent Act 1965, Vol. 18, p. 628.
11. Greek Loan Act 1898, Vol. 22, p. 865.
12. Pensions (Increase) Act 1920, Vol. 24, p. 774.
13. Section 21-23 of the Public Health Act of 1936, Vol. 26, p. 218.
14. Trustee Savings Bank Act 1969, Vol. 30, p. 284.
15. Section 121 of the Town and Country Planning Act 1971, Vol. 41, p. 1726.

ASSIGNMENT 7
ENGLISH STATUTES -- IS IT IN FORCE?

Method:

Using the 1989 edition of Is It In Force? Which accompanies Halsbury's Statutes, find the following Statutes and indicate: a.) If they are currently in force, and b.) if in force, the date of receiving royal assent.

Example

QUESTION: Criminal Justice Act 1972 (c 71).
ANSWER: a.) Yes, in force
b.) RA: 26 Oct. 1972

Questions:

1. Overseas Aid Act 1968 (c57)
2. Dockyard Services Act 1986 (c52)
3. Housing (Scotland) Act 1987 (c26)
4. Mauritius Independence Act 1968 (c8)
5. Broadcast Act 1980 (c64)
6. Trade Union Act 1984 (c49)
7. Tonga Act 1970 (c22)
8. Malicious Communications Act 1988 (c27)
9. Housing (Homeless Persons) Act 1977 (c48)
10. Housing Subsidies Act 1967 (c29)

ASSIGNMENT 8
THE DIGEST - CASE METHOD

Method:

Locate the following case names in Consolidated Table of Cases volumes (1987 reissue). Using the volume number, topic name and the page or case number which you find, locate the digest of the case in question and indicate its citation. If there is more than one citation, give only the first.

Questions:

1. Barner v. Barner (Can.).
2. Bolden v. Brogden (1838).
3. Crewe v. Corbett (N.Z.).
4. Mills v. Edwards (1971).
5. Z. v. Z. (1972) (Aus.).
6. R. v. Rew (1662).
7. Wilson v. Grey (1866).
8. Sheardown v. Good (Can.).
9. Taylor v. Willoughby (1953).
10. Brown v. Nisbett (1750).
11. Gray v. Gray (1852).
12. The Kauss (1904).
13. Kearon v. Kearon (Ir.).
14. Overseas Tankship v. Morts Dock (1961).
15. R. v. Cornwell (1972) (Aus.).

Notes

Notes